HAYDN'S AND MOZART'S SONATA STYLES

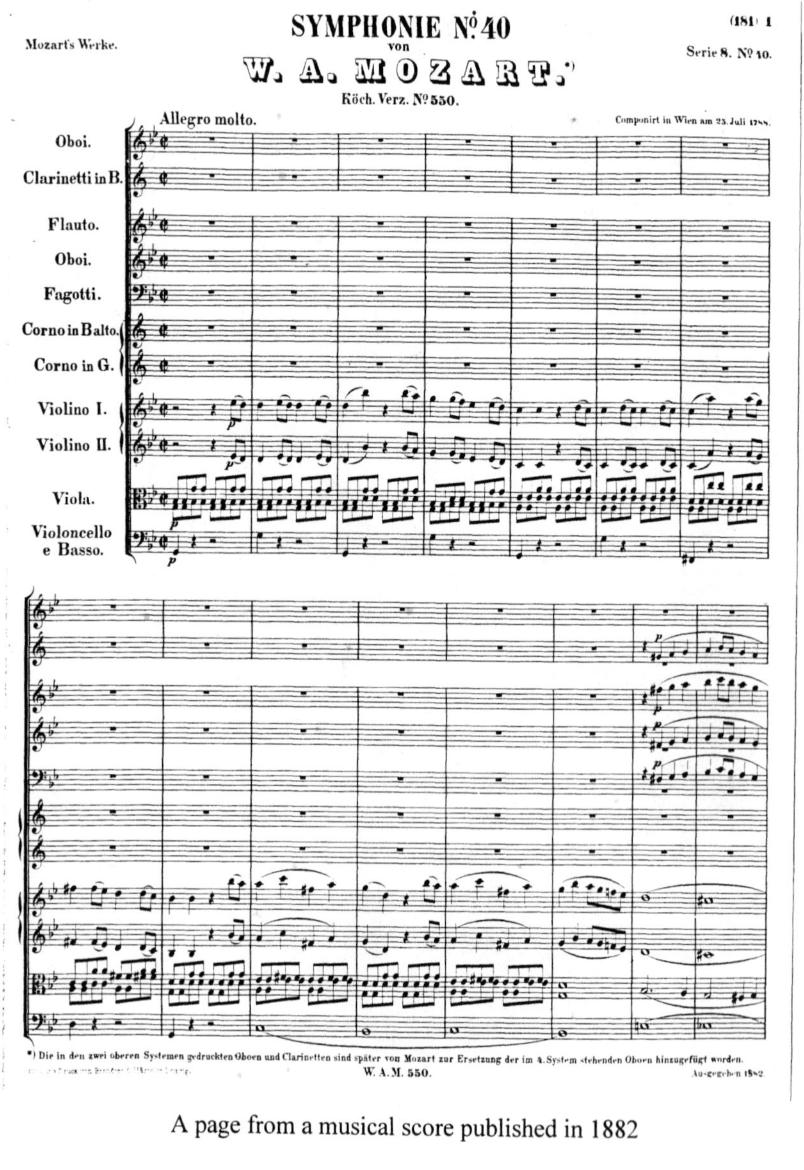

A page from a musical score published in 1882

HAYDN'S AND MOZART'S SONATA STYLES

A Comparison

John Harutunian

Studies in the History and Interpretation of Music
Volume 113

The Edwin Mellen Press
Lewiston•Queenston•Lampeter

Library of Congress Cataloging-in-Publication Data

Harutunian, John Martin, 1948-
   Haydn's and Mozart's sonata styles : a comparison / John Harutunian.
     p. cm. -- (Studies in the history and interpretation of music ; v. 113)
   Includes bibliographical references (p.) and index.
   Contents: Tonic-dominant polarity -- Tonal deflections -- Structural junctures --
Development procedures -- Conclusions.
   ISBN 0-7734-6202-3
    1. Sonata form. 2. Haydn, Joseph, 1732-1809--Criticism and interpretation. 3. Mozart,
Wolfgang Amadeus, 1756-1791--Criticism and interpretation. I. Title. II. Studies in the
history and interpretation of music ; v. 113.

MT62.H37 2005
784.18'3'0922--dc22

                                               2004064996

This is volume 113 in the continuing series
Studies in the History and Interpretation of Music
Volume 113 ISBN 0-7734-6202-3
SHIM Series ISBN 0-88946-426-X

A CIP catalog record for this book is available from the British Library

Front cover: Sketches of Haydn and Mozart by artist Joshua O'Donnell

         The Edwin Mellen Press   The Edwin Mellen Press
                Box 450   Box 67
          Lewiston, New York   Queenston, Ontario
          USA 14092-0450   CANADA L0S 1L0

                  The Edwin Mellen Press, Ltd.
               Lampeter, Ceredigion, Wales
             UNITED KINGDOM SA48 8LT

            Printed in the United States of America

To the memory of the late C.S. Lewis
with highest admiration
and deepest gratitude

Table of Contents

Preface

The names of Franz Joseph Haydn and Wolfgang Amadeus Mozart, like those of Bach and Handel before them and Brahms and Wagner after, are almost inseparably linked. But Haydn and Mozart were more than contemporaries, compatriots, and musical geniuses of the highest order. Unlike their Baroque and Romantic counterparts, their works, in particular their great instrumental compositions, represent more than the twin pinnacles of a central musical tradition; they are, with respect to the High, or Viennese, Classical Style, virtually its exclusive embodiment. As such they arguably constitute the high point of the Western musical tradition altogether.

The critical and scholarly literature devoted to this repertoire is nothing short of oceanic and includes contributions from some of the most profound musical thinkers of the past two centuries – among them such authorities as Hermann Abert, Friedrich Blume, Wilhelm Fischer, Leonard Ratner, Charles Rosen, and Donald Francis Tovey. In consequence we possess a scholarly "canon" roughly commensurate with its towering object. Thanks to their achievements the hallmarks of the Viennese Classical Style are fairly well understood.

This makes it all the more surprising that one fundamental, and embarrassingly obvious, question bearing on the music of Haydn and Mozart has been far less satisfactorily addressed. In light of their shared musical language and aesthetic understanding, what, exactly, makes Haydn's music so palpably different from Mozart's? Every serious musician and music lover is keenly aware of the unmistakable individuality of these two composers. Yet a fully comprehensive attempt to identify its source and to account for it has never before been undertaken.

In the ambitious work presented here John Harutunian provides some of the most perceptive answers offered by anyone in the last thirty years to this perennial challenge to musical criticism. With refreshing, unconcealed enthusiasm and an ear for the significant detail Harutunian offers nothing less than a systematic explication for the uniqueness of musical genius. Concentrating on a few critical issues of formal and tonal design raised by the conventions of eighteenth-century sonata style, Harutunian investigates Haydn's and Mozart's differing approaches to them with admirable specificity. The discussion is generously illustrated with hundreds of musical examples drawn from virtually every pertinent instrumental genre cultivated by the two Viennese masters. Above all, in presenting his argument Harutunian does not fail to inquire into the aesthetic rationale – that is, the intensely personal motivations and strategies – that animated and informed critical compositional decisions.

In sum, all admirers of the music of Franz Joseph Haydn and Wolfgang Amadeus Mozart owe a substantial debt of gratitude to John Harutunian for this landmark of musical scholarship.

Robert L. Marshall
Sachar Professor of Music emeritus
Brandeis University

Foreword

The names of Franz Joseph Haydn and Wolfgang Amadeus Mozart are so closely intertwined that most people speak them in the same breath. They were not only contemporaneous composers, using the harmonic vocabulary of the late eighteenth century at a time when its syntax was the most restricted and defined, but they shared the summit in the development of a procedure we can best refer to today as the sonata style. Nevertheless, experienced listeners can readily distinguish between their idioms. Articulating these differences, however, so as to present a comprehensive picture of the composers' individual styles, is another matter.

This book attempts to present such a picture. In doing so it relies on basic formal concepts and chordal analysis. While the author is aware of other methods of analysis (Schenkerian analysis, motivic approaches, etc.), the present study is intended to lay necessary groundwork for any approach to understanding the distinguishing characteristics of these two great composers. It will draw attention to some phenomena already grasped intuitively by experienced listeners. This is as it should be. Aesthetic perception often begins with intuitive apprehension, and this can lead ultimately to an articulated understanding. To guide this progress is the goal of this book.

Acknowledgments

The initial stimulus for this book came from a casual observation made to me some thirty-five years ago about differences in Haydn's and Mozart's uses of chromaticism. To the author of that observation, Professor (now emeritus) Reginald Gerig of Wheaton (Illinois) College, I would like to express my thanks.

I am especially indebted to the faculty members at UCLA who supervised the dissertation of which this book is a revision, particularly Professor Malcolm Cole for his warm interest and encouragement. Most of all, I am thankful to my advisor, Professor Robert Winter, for his valuable suggestions on both style and content.

I am also indebted to the enormous labors of Michael Kibbe and Vincent Cole in transcribing the legion of musical examples, and to Rebecca Soderman for her diligence in printing them. Special thanks are due to Louise MacDonald for her exceptionally accurate typing of the manuscript.

I am particularly appreciative of the assistance of Alice Klein, who not only compiled the index but also made many insightful editorial suggestions.

A note of thanks is also due to Gordon and Breach Publishers for permission to reprint material which had appeared earlier in another form. (Chapter One is a revised version of "Haydn and Mozart: Tonic-Dominant Polarity in Mature Sonata-Style Works," which appeared in The Journal of Musicological Research, volume 9 [1990], pp. 273-298. The copyright owner is Overseas Publishers Association N.V., with permission from Gordon and Breach Publishers.)

Finally, I am most grateful for the continual love and support of two extremely generous individuals: my parents, John and Karmille Harutunian.

Newton, Massachusetts
October, 2004

Chord Symbols

The chord symbols used in this study are listed below. The keys of C Major and C Minor are used to illustrate the patterns of intervals for the chord types named.

Key: C Major

Name	*Symbol*	*Chord*
Tonic	I	C-E-G
Minor Tonic	i	C-E^b-G
Neapolitan Sixth	N^6	F-A^b-D^b
Supertonic	ii	D-F-A
Diminished Supertonic	ii°	D-F-A^b
Flatted Mediant	III^b	E^b-G-B^b
Mediant	iii	E-G-B
Major Mediant	III	E-G$^\#$-B
Subdominant	IV	F-A-C
Minor Subdominant	iv	F-A^b-C
Augmented Sixth	IV$^{6\#}$	A^b-C-E^b-F$^\#$
Dominant	V	G-B-D
Minor Dominant	v	G-B^b-D
Diminished Dominant	V°	G-B^b-D^b
Flatted Submediant	VI^b	A^b-C-E^b
Submediant	vi	A-C-E
Subtonic	VII^b	B^b-D-F
Leading Tone	vii°	B-D-F
Flatted Tonic	I^b	B-D$^\#$-F$^\#$

Key: C Minor

Name	Symbol	Chord
Tonic	i	C-E$\flat$-G
Major Tonic	I	C-E$\natural$-G
Neapolitan Sixth	N^6	F-A$\flat$-D$\flat$
Subdominant	iv	F-A$\flat$-C
Major Subdominant	IV	F-A$\natural$-C
Dominant	V	G-B$\natural$-D
Submediant	VI	A$\flat$-C-E$\flat$
Leading Tone	vii°	B$\natural$-D-F

The local analysis of a given chord will be denoted throughout by a Roman numeral below the staff, while its long-range significance will be indicated by a numeral between the staves.

Introduction

Central to the music of Haydn and Mozart is the concept of sonata style. Of this there have been innumerable accounts, from Heinrich Christoph Koch in the eighteenth century to Charles Rosen in the twentieth.[1] Nevertheless a brief summary is appropriate here.

A sonata-style movement opens with a section in which the basic material is "exposed," or laid out. This opening section always includes a modulation along the way and therefore ends in a different key from the one it started in. The exposition is followed by a development section, in which the potential of the basic material is worked out as the music courses through various keys. Last comes a recapitulation section, in which the opening material is revisited, but with the important difference that all of it is now heard in the home key, giving a sense of resolution and completion.

In the exposition section of a sonata-style movement, stable opening material appears in the tonic – material which hence is said to occupy the "primary key area." There follows a modulation or "transition" which leads to a second stable plateau ("secondary key area") nearly always in the dominant (or, if the movement is in a minor key, the relative major). Further material (the "closing area"), often involving dominant-tonic reiterations of the secondary key, concludes the exposition. This entire section is generally repeated. The material after the arrival of the dominant is heard as structurally dissonant to the whole.

In the development section that follows, one or more themes from the exposition are subjected to sequential and/or contrapuntal treatment, occasionally with new material introduced. In some movements the development consists largely of conventional material, such as sequential scale patterns and arpeggios.

---

[1]   Respectively, *Versuch einer Anleitung zur Composition* (Leipzig, 1782-93) and *Sonata Forms* (W. W. Norton: New York, 1980), pp. 96-126.

This section culminates in a "retransition," a passage which prepares for the return of the tonic. This is chiefly accomplished via a "pedal point" – a tone sustained in the bass part while the other parts move without reference to it – on the dominant.

The return of the tonic marks the beginning of the third section – the recapitulation – and usually coincides with the reappearance of the opening material. A critical unstable passage follows. Though analogous to the transition in the exposition, it nevertheless ends not by modulating to the dominant but by reasserting the tonic. The secondary area material now returns rewritten (or "retransposed") in the home key, thus resolving the structural dissonance it created in the exposition.[2] (The critical passage which turns the harmonic direction back around toward the tonic may be referred to as an altered transition, a retransposition passage or, more popularly, as a "twist." In the writer's opinion, "adjustment" is the most felicitous term.) Following the secondary area material, closing material returns, also transposed back into the tonic. At the end of the recapitulation repeat marks may appear, calling for a repetition of both development and recapitulation. There may also be a final coda, whose function is to round out harmonic and thematic processes begun earlier.[3]

The normative aspect of this outline should not obscure the flexibility of sonata style. Haydn and Mozart were faced not with stiff formal schemes but with an infinite variety of possibilities, which they explored in such depth and breadth as to imbue every one of their movements with a dramatic interest that remains as vital today as it was in the eighteenth century.

---

[2]   The term "retransposition" is admittedly awkward. Its underlying rationale involves the postulation of an abstract Tonic as a sort of metaphysical ground for all of the material of a movement. Hence the initial appearance of the secondary area material in the dominant already represents a "transposition," and its later recurrence in the tonic a "retransposition." The term is entirely appropriate, however, when used in connection with concerto procedure: the latter part of the opening orchestral introduction, or ritornello, reappears "transposed" to the dominant in the solo part later in the exposition, and hence is indeed "retransposed" when it returns in the tonic in the recapitulation.

[3]   A variant of this procedure is sonata-rondo, in which the opening material returns in the tonic between the exposition and the development, and again at the very end. Thus melodic and harmonic recurrence weaken large-scale dramatic tension. This procedure remains outside the scope of this study.

A General Overview of Research

Only a few scholars have attempted systematic comparisons of Haydn and Mozart. The most respected among them is Friedrich Blume.[4] However, Blume's reluctance to move beyond generalities limits the value of his study. For example, he states that Mozart, in his symphonic production, first shows Haydn's influence in his last three Salzburg symphonies: K. 318, 319, and 338 (p. 577). He cites thematic development, counterpoint, minuets more highly developed than in previous symphonies, variation technique, and a tendency toward cyclic unity ("streben nach zyklischer Einheit"). He cites no specific passages, however, and his reference to "cyclic unity" is particularly obscure: he may be referring to K. 318, written as one continuous ABA movement; K. 319, whose first, third, and fourth movements all begin with phrases outlining a tonic-dominant-tonic progression; or K. 338, whose first and last movements both start with a descending octave leap followed by melodic ascent. In any case, "cyclic unity" does seem to overstate the evidence.[5] Blume states further that Haydn's influence is even more evident in Mozart's last six symphonies, but the sole evidence he provides is the monothematicism of the "Haffner" Symphony. With respect to Mozart's influence on Haydn, he cites the "Paris" Symphonies, particularly their treatment of the woodwinds. It is not known, he points out, whether Haydn ever heard Mozart's final symphonic trilogy; nothing in the "London" Symphonies suggests that he was familiar with it.

Blume's discussion of the chamber music is also vague. He remarks that Mozart's mature quartets are Haydnesque in their counterpoint, in the overall

---

[4]   "Haydn und Mozart," in *Syntagma Musicologicum: Gesammelte Reden und Schriften* (Kassel: Bärenreiter, 1963), pp. 570-82.

[5]   See Jan LaRue, "Significant and Coincidental Resemblances between Classical Themes," *Journal of the American Musicological Society*, XIV, 1 (1961), pp. 224-34.

structure of their slow movements, minuets, and trios, and in their "cyclic" nature – again without citing specific works (pp. 579-80). In a final paragraph, he concludes with a rejection of the thesis that Mozart foreshadowed Romanticism to a greater degree than Haydn. As evidence he cites the opinions of late-eighteenth- and early-nineteenth-century writers who, he implies, were divided equally on the question. Unfortunately, he does not provide any thoroughgoing stylistic analysis of the music itself.

In contrast to Blume, Hans Engel, in "Haydn, Mozart und die Klassik,"[6] furnishes a rich supply of musical examples to support his points. Dealing exclusively with symphonies, and focusing especially on melody, Engel discusses the concept of dualism within a Classical theme: the juxtaposition of a loud, tutti antecedent phrase (often outlining a triad) and a soft consequent phrase (p. 61).[7] While Haydn generally avoids this type of melodic construction, Mozart employs it in fully half of his symphonic first movements, the most famous instance being the opening of the "Jupiter" Symphony. (Engel lists the symphonies in which he claims to find this characteristic, but a number of them, such as K. 319 and the "Prague" Symphony, do not in fact use it.) He discusses Haydn's frequent use of primary material on arriving at the secondary key area (instances of the monothematic principle at work); he points out that since the theme is transposed and frequently altered, this is in effect a "developmental" procedure (p. 62). Mozart, however, avoids this practice (with some exceptions, one must add, such as the "Haffner" Symphony).

In secondary area themes, Engel argues, Mozart's early symphonies (through K. 162) continue a pre-Classical practice of sounding a melody in parallel thirds over a pedal point. But Mozart is the more "progressive" composer in the way he begins his developments. While Haydn's early symphonies (specifically Nos. 1-27) simply repeat the opening material in the dominant – in the typical pre-Classical manner – Mozart uses new material or, occasionally, altered material at this point. Yet Engel discusses developments only briefly (pp.

---

6   *Mozart-Jahrbuch* (1959), pp. 46-79.

7   As Engel notes, earlier writers have stressed this concept, especially Robert Sondheimer in "Die Sinfonien Franz Becks," *Zeitschrift für Musikwissenschaft*, IV, 8 (1922), pp. 449-84.

65-66), contrasting Haydn's workmanlike thoroughness with Mozart's greater freedom. He is also rather cursory in his treatment of recapitulations, noting Haydn's frequent formal changes in contrast to Mozart's symmetry. Engel concludes with four pages of incipits from first and last movements in Haydn's and Mozart's early symphonies. These are meant to demonstrate thematic relationships between the movements; they are not, however, uniformly convincing.[8]

Engel's study is a valuable one, but it exhibits two principal defects. First is his stress on melodic elements, to the point where harmony – a crucial element in Classical sonata style – is thrust into the background. Second is his heavy concentration on the early and middle symphonies of both composers. Granting the value of tracing Haydn's and Mozart's developments as symphonists, his virtual omission of any treatment of Haydn's "London" Symphonies or Mozart's last six is nevertheless conspicuous to say the least, since his title leads the reader to expect some discussion of the fully developed symphonic style of High Classicism.

A strong historical emphasis appears in Wilhelm Fischer's "Zur Entwicklungsgeschichte des Wiener Klassischen Stils" ("The Historical Development of the Viennese Classical Style").[9] Fischer's discussion of Baroque *Fortspinnung* ("spinning out") and Classical *Lied* ("song") types, a pioneering effort in its day, is still highly valuable. His observations on Haydn and Mozart are well documented. He notes that Mozart's symphonies, in addition to using a contrasting theme in the secondary area, often include a reference to the opening theme as part of the closing area (a famous example is the opening movement of the Symphony No. 40). Haydn, however, often repeats the opening material on arriving in the dominant, bringing in a contrasting theme only in the closing

---

[8]   One of these demonstrations purports to show a thematic relationship between the outer movements of Mozart's K. 338. Since the work is one of the three symphonies cited by Friedrich Blume for its "cyclic unity," this may be a source for Blume's statement. On its own merits the link is not particularly convincing.

[9]   *Studien zur Musikwissenschaft*, II (1915), pp. 24-84.

area.[10] This theme is often a *Lied* type (i.e., showing periodic phrasing), as in Symphonies Nos. 94, 96, 97, 99, 101, and 103.[11] With regard to piano sonatas, Fischer notes Haydn's greater freedom in their overall format; Mozart's usual fast-slow-fast pattern appears in only half of Haydn's sonatas (pp. 68-69). Mozart's slow movements are usually in the subdominant, occasionally in the dominant; Haydn also favors the subdominant and dominant, but frequently uses the tonic minor also. Unfortunately, Fischer does not discuss Classical chamber music.

Fischer's study, like Engel's, proceeds on the assumption that thematic structure, rather than harmony, is the crucial element in Classical sonata style. In view of the date of his article (1915), Fischer's misconception is understandable. He was writing in the twilight of Romanticism, when theorists (and composers!) conceived of "sonata form" as a melodic rather than as a harmonic scheme.[12]

A highly sophisticated, though hardly thoroughgoing, foray into sonata style is found in Charles Rosen's landmark study, *The Classical Style* (1971, expanded edition 1997).[13] Rosen's highly original and iconoclastic approach perhaps did more to rekindle interest in a long-familiar musical style than any other effort in the twentieth century.[14] A central tenet of Rosen's approach is the contrast he makes between Mozart's mastery of operatic form and Haydn's relative lack of success in this genre, this in spite of Haydn's fondness for explicitly dramatic effects (e.g., sudden modulations). Further, notes Rosen, Haydn's melodies are less conventional, more "immediately descriptive of a

---

[10]   P. 59. As his source he cites Heinrich Jalowetz, "Beethoven's Jugendwerke in ihren melodischen Beziehungen zu Mozart, Haydn und Ph. E. Bach," *Sammelbände der Internationalen Musikgesellschaft*, Leipzig: Breitkopf & Härtel, XII (1910-1911), p. 422.

[11]   Fischer uses the old numbering: London Symphony No. 1, etc.

[12]   Charles Rosen, *The Classical Style* (New York: W. W. Norton, 1997), pp. 30-31.

[13]   New York: W.W. Norton.

[14]   See the reviews by Edward T. Cone in *The New York Times Book Review*, May 23, 1971, pp. 34-35; William H. Youngren in *The Hudson Review*, XXV, 1972-73, pp. 633-46; Alan Tyson in *The New York Review of Books*, XVIII, June 15, 1972, pp. 10-12; and B. H. Haggin in *The Sewanee Review*, LXXXI, Spring 1973, pp. 356-64.

specific sentiment or action" than Mozart's, a quality that reaches its peak in the "tone-painting" and "sentiment painting" of *The Creation* and *The Seasons* (p. 185). Why then did Mozart have greater success with opera?

For Rosen the answer lies in Mozart's superior handling of long-range tonal relations, in his capacity to treat tonality "as a mass, a large area of energy which can encompass and resolve the most contradictory opposing forces" (p. 186). (An ideal example is the first movement of the "Jupiter" Symphony.) This enables him "to slow down the purely formal harmonic scheme of his music so that it [does] not outstrip the action on the stage." Mozart's long-range tonal stability, then, provides a "frame of reference" to which he relates his subsidiary tonalities. Unlike Haydn, whose opening material is more unstable, "more immediately charged with a dynamic movement away from the tonic" (as in the opening of the String Quartet Op. 33, No. 4), Mozart's openings are "solidly based" – for example the first movement of the String Quartet K. 428, whose initial octave leap on the tonic supplies a tonal frame for the chromaticism of the following measures. Finally, Rosen notes that Haydn's expositions, in addition to their tonal instability, have marked nervous energy. Haydn, then, must make greater structural changes in his recapitulations in order to provide a stable conclusion. In contrast, "Mozart's more massive treatment of the tonal areas of the exposition often results in recapitulations that are symmetrically equivalent..." Hence Mozart's music, unlike Haydn's, reflects "a state of constant balance" (p. 187).

Yet Rosen's treatment of the Classical style is not without its gaps. Having acknowledged Haydn's large-scale changes in his recapitulations, he omits any discussion of them (except for brief, scattered references, such as the formal expansion found in the "Oxford" Symphony [pp. 160-62]). If, as Rosen himself points out, "the classical style is a style of reinterpretation" (p. 78), his relative silence on this important stylistic aspect is conspicuous indeed, especially with a composer like Haydn, for whom frequent and often major changes are a salient feature of his music. The book also reveals a gap in its treatment of Mozart. Noting his sensitivity to long-range tonal relations and resultant mastery of operatic requirements (pp. 185-86), Rosen offers little discussion of this sensitivity as it applies to his purely instrumental music. Yet it is an important feature of Mozart's style – not only in piano concerti and string quintets, but also in symphonies and string quartets, two important genres of his works which Rosen largely omits.

A more recent study by Rosen, *Sonata Forms* (1980),[15] though more didactic in style and schematic in format, is again stimulating and superbly written. In it Rosen relates sonata style to the more prominent social function of instrumental music in the mid-eighteenth century, and to the shift in aesthetics away from the "notion of music as an imitation of sentiment" and towards "the conception of music as an independent system that conveyed its own significance..." (p. 11). He traces the origins of sonata style from the Baroque aria and concerto, describes the various "sonata forms" of the second half of the eighteenth century, and discusses the style's evolution towards High Classicism. After dealing with motif and function, he devotes a chapter to each of the three sections of a sonata-style movement: exposition, development, and recapitulation, signifying opposition, intensification, and resolution. He concludes with discussions of nineteenth- and twentieth-century works.

With regard to Haydn-Mozart differences, however, Rosen limits himself to a few scattered points. He mentions Mozart's transitions, where the modulation often results "from the introduction of new material or from the introduction of unexpected dissonance into the counterstatement of the opening theme" (p. 232). This contrasts with Haydn, who "often repeatedly emphasized a dissonant element in the main theme until it produced the modulation for him." Rosen notes that these two methods "demand different kinds of thematic material and result in different arrangements of texture." He also observes that Mozart, on arriving at the dominant, more frequently presents an "opposition of themes" (p. 229) – presumably referring to their contrast in character with those of the tonic area – and that his secondary areas reveal a greater variety of expressive themes in general (p. 230).

Neither of Rosen's volumes, then, systematically explores Haydn-Mozart differences. In particular, *The Classical Style* – the more broadly conceptual of the two studies – raises a critical issue generally overlooked: Is Mozart's stronger emphasis on tonal dissonance and resolution at the broadest level related to any other aspects of his style? For example, does it imply comparative harmonic

---

15   New York: W.W. Norton.

stability at a purely local level? If so, does this stability appear at specific junctures in the music – e.g., as continuity of key at the exposition-development break? How does his long-range emphasis affect the overall structure of his movements? Are Mozart's developments best understood as essentially expanded retransitions, which serve to prepare the tonal resolution back to the tonic? How does the long-range emphasis affect Mozart's use of tonal deflections? If such passages disturb harmonic stability in the exposition, does Mozart ever resolve the instability by altering the deflection when it recurs in the recapitulation, so as to produce greater harmonic relaxation? In other words: How far will Mozart go in subordinating formal symmetry to resolution of long-range tension?

In both studies, Rosen's omissions are easily understandable. *The Classical Style* is not only a stylistic but also an historical study, and Rosen rightly focuses on those aspects of Classical style whose development evidences historical continuity – for example the rise of periodic phrasing (previously confined to dance suites), the concept of a sonata-style movement as a series of dramatic events (first appearing in the sonatas of Domenico Scarlatti, p. 43), and the practice of large-scale transposition of material into the tonic in recapitulations. *Sonata Forms*, though containing more detailed analyses, also deals with the movement of a style through history. Rosen is not so much concerned with the differences between the sonata styles of Haydn and Mozart as he is with differences between these two composers on the one hand and Schubert, for example, on the other. With regard to Haydn-Mozart differences, then, both of these volumes are suggestive rather than comprehensive.

A long-awaited scholarly study, in some ways an historical antidote to Rosen's more stylistic approach, is Leonard Ratner's *Classic Music: Expression, Form and Style* (1980).[16] The comprehensiveness which the title implies is fully evident in this impressive work. Ratner examines the Classical repertoire employing four broad areas of inquiry: a) expression, including such varied dimensions as dance and march types, the singing style, and storm and stress; b) rhetoric, including periodicity, harmony, rhythm, melody, texture, and performance; c) form, including sonata form, aria, concerto, etc.; and d) stylistic perspectives, including national styles, serious and comic styles, and brief

---

16   New York: Schirmer Books.

9

treatments of Haydn, Mozart, and Beethoven. Drawing extensively on the writings of eighteenth-century theorists, Ratner nevertheless avoids dry schematization; his lucid style and abundant musical illustrations are strong assets. Yet for a reader interested specifically in comparisons between Haydn and Mozart, the book is of little value. None of the theoretical passages cited discusses the subject, and of the sections devoted to the two composers, each deals exclusively with a single work (Haydn's Piano Sonata H. XVI, No. 52, and Mozart's *Don Giovanni*). Hence, the whole subject of stylistic comparison is bypassed.

From this review of the literature, it is clear that many questions remain to be answered about sonata style in Haydn and Mozart. The present work is an attempt to do so. It is a systematic comparison of the sonata-style procedures of the two composers as found in the mature examples of their major instrumental genres. Five stylistic dimensions have been selected for analysis: tonic-dominant polarity, tonal deflections, harmonic language at structural junctures, development procedures, and recapitulation procedures.

The first of these, tonic-dominant polarity, is the sense of implicit distance, opposition, and tension between the two basic tonal forces. A salient feature of Classical tonality, this polarity makes possible the drama of sonata style. The motion from tonic to dominant, the arrival in the dominant, and the ultimate return to the tonic all have dramatic significance – determined at least in part by this polarization of tonal forces. The crucial question is: Can this polarity be measured? If so, is it greater in one composer than in the other?

The second dimension, tonal deflections, involves momentary deviations from the overall tonal plan. Their frequency, length, and remoteness of key constitute one measure of a composer's harmonic freedom. Here the basic question involves function: Can these deflections be explained in terms of larger harmonic goals? Does their material ever recur elsewhere in the movement? Do these passages reveal differences in practice between Haydn and Mozart?

The third stylistic dimension involves the nature of harmonic language at structural junctures, revealing the basic manner of large-scale formal articulation. The first such point is the exposition-development break. How dramatic is the articulation here? Is there a sudden modulation, or is the effect of the break attenuated by harmonic continuity? The second is the development-recapitulation juncture. Here the crucial issue of course involves retransitions. How long are they? Are they invariably centered on the dominant, implying the composer's concern for resolution of long-range harmonic tension? Or may they occur on other tonal centers as well?

Development procedures constitute the fourth area. Here there is no proscribed harmonic plan; the composer's imagination has free rein. Given such freedom, any differences in procedure are especially revealing. Which composer favors greater continuity? Who writes more sectionalized developments, i. e., interrupts sequential texture with stable tonal plateaus? Does this imply a basic conceptual difference regarding the development as it relates to the overall structure?

Finally, recapitulation procedures represent a crucial area of stylistic differentiation. The questions they raise involve symmetry: Are these sections basically repetitions of exposition material with only ornamental changes, or do they involve major alterations of structure? If the latter, would this not suggest an underlying principle of sonata style as "continuous development"?

By focusing on these dimensions of style, the author's goal is to illuminate the relationship between these two masters.

List of Repertoire

The following works form the basis for the present study. They include all sonata-style movements found within the major instrumental genres of Haydn and Mozart beginning with the year 1781. This is the year generally acknowledged as marking Haydn's ultimate arrival, with his String Quartets Opus 33, at the High Classical style. Slow movements, movements in minor keys, and movements without developments are indicated as such.

Haydn: Symphonies

		Slow movement	*Minor key*	*No development*
No. 82 ("L'Ours")	First movement			
	Fourth movement			
No. 83 ("La Poule")	First movement		minor	
	Second movement	slow		
	Fourth movement			
No. 84	First movement			
	Fourth movement			
No. 85 ("La Reine")	First movement			
No. 86	First movement			
	Second movement	slow		
	Fourth movement			
No. 87	First movement			
	Second movement	slow		
	Fourth movement			
No. 88	First movement			
	Second movement	slow		no dev
No. 89	First movement			
No. 90	First movement			
	Fourth movement			
No. 91	First movement			
	Fourth movement			

No. 92 ("Oxford")	First movement			
	Second movement	slow		
	Fourth movement			
No. 93	First movement			
	Fourth movement			
No. 94 ("Surprise")	First movement			
No. 95	First movement		minor	
	Fourth movement			
No. 96 ("Miracle")	First movement			
No. 97	First movement			
No. 98	First movement			
	Second movement	slow		
	Fourth movement			
No. 99 ("Imperial")	First movement			
	Second movement	slow		
No. 100 ("Military")	First movement			
	Fourth movement			
No. 101 ("Clock")	First movement			
No. 102	First movement			
No. 103 ("Drumroll")	First movement			
No. 104 ("London")	First movement			
	Fourth movement			

Haydn: String Quartets
Op. 33 ("Gli Scherzi" or "Russian" Quartets)

No. 1	First movement		minor	
	Third movement	slow		
	Fourth movement		minor	
No. 2 ("Joke")	First movement			
No. 3 ("Bird")	First movement			
	Third movement	slow		no dev
	Fourth movement			
No. 4	First movement			
	Third movement	slow		no dev
No. 5	First movement			
	Second movement	slow	minor	no dev
No. 6	First movement			
	Second movement	slow	minor	no dev

Op. 42

	First movement	minor	
	Fourth movement	minor	

Op. 50 ("Prussian" Quartets)

No. 1	First movement		
	Fourth movement		
No. 2	First movement		
	Second movement	slow	no dev
	Fourth movement		
No. 3	First movement		
	Fourth movement		
No. 4	First movement	minor	
No. 5	First movement		
	Second movement	slow	no dev
	Fourth movement		
No. 6 ("Frog")	First movement		
	Second movement	slow	minor
	Fourth movement		

Op. 54

No. 1	First movement	
	Second movement	slow
No. 2	First movement	
No. 3	First movement	
	Fourth movement	

Op. 55

No. 1	First movement		
	Second movement	slow	no dev
No. 2	Second movement	minor	
	Fourth movement		
No. 3	First movement		
	Fourth movement		

Op. 64

No. 1	First movement		
	Fourth movement		
No. 2	First movement	minor	
	Fourth movement	minor	

No. 3	First movement			
	Fourth movement			
No. 4	First movement			
	Fourth movement			
No. 5 ("Lark")	First movement			
No. 6	First movement			

Op. 71

No. 1	First movement			
	Fourth movement			
No. 2	First movement			
	Second movement	slow		
No. 3	First movement			

Op. 74

No. 1	First movement			
	Second movement	slow		
	Fourth movement			
No. 2	First movement			
	Fourth movement			
No. 3 ("Rider")	First movement		minor	
	Fourth movement		minor	

Op. 76

No. 1	First movement			
	Second movement	slow		no dev
	Fourth movement		minor	
No. 2 ("Quinten")	First movement		minor	
	Fourth movement		minor	
No. 3 ("Emperor")	First movement			
	Fourth movement		minor	
No. 4 ("Sunrise")	First movement			
	Second movement	slow		no dev
No. 5	Second movement	slow		
	Fourth movement			
No. 6	Fourth movement			

Op. 77

No. 1	First movement			
	Second movement	slow		
	Fourth movement			

No. 2	First movement			
	Fourth movement			

Haydn: Piano Trios, H. XV

No. 5	First movement	slow		no dev
	Second movement			
No. 6	First movement			
No. 8	First movement			
No. 9	First movement	slow		
	Second movement			
No. 10	First movement			
	Second movement			
No. 11	First movement			
No. 12	First movement		minor	
	Second movement	slow		
No. 13	Second movement			
No. 14	First movement			
No. 15	First movement			
No. 16	First movement			
	Second movement	slow	minor	
No. 17	First movement			
	Second movement			
No. 18	First movement			
	Third movement			no dev
No. 19	Second movement	slow		no dev
	Third movement		minor	
No. 20	First movement			
No. 21	First movement			
	Third movement			
No. 22	First movement			
	Second movement	slow		
	Third movement			
No. 23	Second movement	slow		no dev
	Third movement			
No. 24	First movement			
No. 26	First movement		minor	
No. 27	First movement			
	Third movement			
No. 28	First movement			
	Second movement		minor	no dev
No. 29	Third movement			

No. 30	First movement		
	Second movement	slow	no dev
No. 32	Second movement		

Haydn: Piano Sonatas, H. XVI

No. 34	First movement		minor
	Second movement	slow	
No. 41	First movement		
No. 43	First movement		
No. 49	First movement		
No. 50	First movement		
	Second movement	slow	no dev
	Third movement		
No. 51	First movement		
	Second movement		
No. 52	First movement		
	Third movement		

Haydn Total: 174 movements

Mozart: Symphonies

		Slow movement	Minor key	No development
No. 35, K. 385	First movement			
("Haffner")	Second movement	slow		
No. 36, K. 425	First movement			
("Linz")	Second movement	slow		
	Fourth movement			
No. 38, K. 504	First movement			
("Prague")	Second movement	slow		
	Third movement			
No. 39, K. 543	First movement			
	Second movement	slow		no dev
	Fourth movement			
No. 40, K. 550	First movement		minor	
	Second movement	slow		
	Fourth movement		minor	
No. 41, K. 551	First movement			
("Jupiter")	Second movement	slow		
	Fourth movement			

18

Mozart: String Quartets

No. 14, K. 387	First movement			
	Third movement	slow		no dev
	Fourth movement			
No. 15, K. 421	First movement		minor	
No. 16, K. 428	First movement			
	Second movement	slow		
	Fourth movement			no dev
No. 17, K. 458	First movement			
	Third movement	slow		no dev
	Fourth movement			
No. 18, K. 464	First movement			
	Fourth movement			
No. 19, K. 465	First movement			
("Dissonant")	Second movement	slow		no dev
	Fourth movement			
No. 20, K. 499	First movement			
("Hoffmeister")	Third movement	slow		
	Fourth movement			
No. 21, K. 575	First movement			
No. 22, K. 589	First movement			
	Second movement	slow		no dev
	Fourth movement			
No. 23, K. 590	First movement			
	Second movement	slow		
	Fourth movement			

Mozart: Quintets

K. 406 (String)	First movement		minor	
	Second movement	slow		
K. 407	First movement			
	Second movement	slow		
K. 515 (String)	First movement			
	Third movement	slow		no dev
K. 516 (String)	First movement		minor	
	Third movement	slow		no dev
K. 581 (Clarinet)	First movement			
K. 593 (String)	First movement			
	Second movement	slow		
	Fourth movement			

K. 614 (String)	First movement		

Mozart: Piano Sonatas

K. 333	First movement		
	Second movement	slow	
K. 457	First movement		minor
K. 533 and 494	First movement		
	Second movement	slow	
K. 545	First movement		
K. 547a	First movement		
K. 570	First movement		
K. 576	First movement		
	Second movement	slow	no dev

Mozart: Piano Concerti

No. 11, K. 413	First movement			
	Second movement	slow		no dev
No. 12, K. 414	First movement			
	Second movement	slow		
No. 13, K. 415	First movement			
	Second movement	slow		no dev
No. 14, K. 449	First movement			
	Second movement	slow		
No. 15, K. 450	First movement			
No. 16, K. 451	First movement			
No. 17, K. 453	First movement			
No. 18, K. 456	First movement			
No. 19, K. 459	First movement			
	Second movement	slow		no dev
No. 20, K. 466	First movement		minor	
No. 21, K. 467	First movement			
	Second movement	slow		
No. 22, K. 482	First movement			
No. 23, K. 488	First movement			
No. 24, K. 491	First movement		minor	
No. 25, K. 503	First movement			
	Second movement	slow		no dev
No. 26, K. 537	First movement			
No. 27, K. 595	First movement			

Mozart Total: 89 movements

Chapter One

Tonic-Dominant Polarity

The Classical style was above all dramatic. Quite unlike the smooth continuity of a Baroque fugue or dance movement is the articulated series of events that constitutes a Classic piece. Naturally, the new style did not develop overnight.[17] But even as Bach and Handel were creating the masterworks that were the final glories of the Baroque era, one of their contemporaries was leading music in a very different direction.

Domenico Scarlatti (born 1685) began in the 1720s to write harpsichord sonatas which proved to be harbingers of things to come. By the time of his death in 1757 he had written 555 such pieces. L. 415, a case in point, opens with a trumpet-like fanfare:

Scarlatti: Sonata in D, L. 415

The tonic pedal point heightens the proclamatory quality of the opening phrase. Scarlatti is announcing the series of musical events that will form the

[17]   The seminal study tracing its development is Wilhelm Fischer's "Zur Entwicklungsgeschichte des Wiener Klassichen Stils," *Studien zur Musikwissenschaft* III (1915), pp. 24-84.

exposition.[18] These follow in due course: an imitation of clicking castanets,

a modulation to the dominant that winds up with a dramatic flourish,

a new syncopated melody in the minor dominant,

[18]   See the succinct discussion in *A History of Western Music* by Donald J. Grout and Claude V. Palisca, 5th edition, W. W. Norton: New York, 1996, pp. 470-71.

the strumming of a guitar – with a reiterated dissonant A suggesting an open string,

the reappearance of the castanets, and then a concluding passage featuring crossed hands in a brilliantly effective display:

But there is more to the last passage than mere brilliance. The reiterated alternations of tonic and dominant create something previously unknown in music: a clever "play of opposites" effect. This assertive wittiness is a new element in musical style. And the assertiveness is bound up with the new-found identities of the chords themselves. No longer simple mechanisms of local tension and resolution, they now represent opposite poles of harmonic meaning. As the eighteenth century ran its course, the distance between the poles steadily increased. Eventually it widened to such a point that such reiterations expressed tension and conflict. By the time Beethoven was writing his mature masterworks, block-chord alternations of tonic and dominant were capable of expressing the fist-shaking dramatic gesture inevitably associated with that musical titan.

This kind of gesture is not generally identified with Haydn and Mozart. Nevertheless, beneath the surface of this chord progression there lies a deeper issue: the ability of the tonic and dominant poles to control large areas of a piece of music, to support blocks of musical material which are structurally dissonant with each other – in short, the concept of the harmonically dissonant *section*.[19] It is this structural harmonic polarity which gives the Classical style its continuous operatic tension, a tension found not only in Beethoven but in Haydn and Mozart as well. The move to the dominant at the transition, the return home to the tonic at the start of the recapitulation, and the final affirmation of the tonic at the critical harmonic adjustment are the three overarching events in a sonata-style movement. Their significance is closely bound up with the distance between the two tonal poles. A measurement of this distance would reveal much about Haydn's and Mozart's concepts of musical drama.

Fortunately, there are two stylistic dimensions which may serve as yardsticks. One is the strength of the move to the dominant. The more emphatic the modulation, the greater the polarity – and hence the more dramatic the arrival of the dominant.

In the finale of Haydn's Symphony No. 84, the strength of the modulation results in part from its sheer length. The critical harmonic progression occurs at bars 32-34:

---

[19]   See Charles Rosen's *The Classical Style* (W. W. Norton: New York, 1997), p. 26.

+Bass 8va

E♭ ⟶ B♭

Haydn: Symphony No. 84, fourth movement

V₆/V   V₆

By bar 34, the requirement of a modulation has already been fulfilled, as the new key is now prepared. Yet in order to completely erase the tonic from the listener's memory, Haydn prolongs the agitation for another twenty-nine measures, complete with changes in dynamics and texture, and a sudden chromatic intrusion at bar 56:

After such a prolonged dramatic preparation, the arrival of the secondary area at bar 64 (even though not articulated by a pause) is a harmonic event of the first order. The new tonal world of the dominant is in serious rivalry with that of the tonic, with all of the tension and opposition that such a rivalry implies. The polarization of forces is strong.

In the finale of the String Quartet Op. 50, No. 2, Haydn gives strength to his modulation through sheer reiteration of the dominant-of-the-dominant-to-dominant progression. (For an explanation of chord symbols see table, pages *vii-viii*.) The insistent, forceful gesture sounds quite unlike Mozart:

Haydn: String Quartet, Op. 50, No. 2, fourth movement

Sometimes Haydn goes a step further and reiterates a progression involving the dominant of the dominant of the dominant, as if to deliberately dramatize the crossing of a tonal boundary (as in the String Quartet Op. 71, No. 2, bars 24-25). Or he has recourse to more sophisticated procedures, as in the finale of the String Quartet Op. 54, No. 2. After using a sequential progression which reduces the status of the tonic to that of a passing chord (bar 39), he sets up the dominant through several forceful reiterations. He then writes a six-bar descending chromatic sequence which not only obliterates any lingering memory of the tonic but establishes a new harmonic perspective – one in which the dominant is seen as a stable point of repose.[20]

---

[20]   He follows a similar procedure in Op. 76, No. 1, where the tonicizing progressions are heard over a pedal point (bars 42-47).

If Haydn's transitions display such individual touches, Mozart's unselfconscious ease in modulating shows a lesser emphasis on this aspect of the form. In the finale of the "Linz" Symphony the transition is quite brief. At measures 39-45, Mozart underplays the approach of the rival key, as the rather tentative motion toward the dominant belies the importance of this impending tonal center:

Mozart: Symphony No. 36, K. 425 ("Linz"), fourth movement

The leading tone-of-the-dominant-of-the-dominant chord at bar 45 is particularly revealing. The critical root, C-sharp, appears as a mere melodic detail carrying little harmonic weight. Though the modulation gains strength in the bars that follow, its harmonic reiterations seem almost cursory when compared to those of Haydn in his Op. 50, No. 2 (bars 32-49), above. And when Mozart's secondary area arrives (bar 58), a sense of dramatic harmonic opposition to the tonic is largely absent; in its place is a stronger melodic emphasis.

Still more direct is Mozart's procedure in the second movement of the "Haffner" Symphony. The lesser tonic-dominant polarity of slow movements in general, where large-scale dramatic tension is minimized in favor of expressive melodic details, gives rise to the appearance of a special device in this piece. The primary area material concludes with a half cadence on the dominant (bar 16), and is followed immediately by the secondary area – there simply is no transition:

Mozart: Symphony No. 35, K. 385 ("Haffner"), second movement

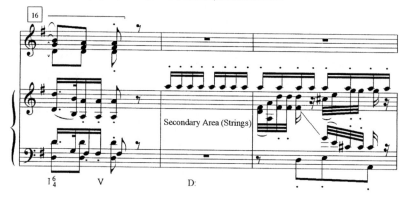

Although the following passage returns briefly to the tonic, creating an oscillating tonic-dominant pattern, the new melodic contour of the above excerpt – and its stable diatonic harmony – clearly mark it as the beginning of the secondary area. When the passage returns in the recapitulation, now of course transposed to the tonic, it is nevertheless "prepared" by exactly the same material:

Hence the half cadence at bar 16 is a "bifocal close:" its harmonic focus allows for subsequent material whose tonality is either "proximate" (the tonic) or more distant (the dominant).[21]

One might think that the summary omission of a transition – a major dimension of sonata style – implied a basic conceptual distinction, i.e., a difference in kind between pieces featuring bifocal closes and conventional ones with transitions. Actually, Mozart's practice involves points on a continuum. Nevertheless, over a dozen movements stand out from his *oeuvre* as making distinct use of this device, though in various modifications. In the slow movement of the Piano Sonata K. 333, Mozart camouflages the procedure with connecting motifs in the bass (at bars 13 and 63), while in several other movements (the opening movements of the String Quartets K. 575 and 590, and the slow movement of K. 428) he assigns the secondary material a partially transitional function.[22]

---

[21]   The term "bifocal close" was first used by Lawrence Bernstein in a graduate seminar at the University of Chicago in 1969, and subsequently adopted by Robert Winter in a paper delivered in 1981.

[22]   Mozart's other bifocal closes all evidence some irregularity of procedure. In two instances – the Piano Concerto K. 449 and the Piano Sonata K. 576 – Mozart modifies the close by adjusting the material that precedes it in the recapitulation. The adjusted versions incorporate harmonies lying on the flat side of the tonic: the resulting change in tonal focus helps anchor the music to the home key. In the slow movements of the Piano Concerti K. 414 and 503, Mozart omits the first half of the secondary area at the recapitulation. In the slow movement of the String Quintet K. 593, the bifocal close is followed initially by secondary material in the minor dominant (the material is transposed to the minor tonic at the recapitulation). This further prepares for the arrival of the major dominant. Mozart thereby compensates for the weak polarity implied by the bifocal close; since the passage in the minor prepares for the ultimate tonal goal, the final attainment of this goal carries a weight it would otherwise lack. The procedure reappears in the Piano Concerto K. 537, where it is subtly varied: the secondary material wavers between major and minor, resulting in the striking emotional ambivalence unique to Mozart's style. (An oblique approach to the dominant also appears in the Piano Sonata K. 547a. The bifocal close is followed

These instances of the bifocal close occur, of course, in only a fraction of Mozart's works. Yet the device is even rarer in Haydn. It occurs unmodified in two pieces, the Piano Sonata H. XVI, No. 41, and the second movement of the Piano Trio H. XV, No. 19. Two other cases document a free adaptation of the procedure. In the Piano Sonata H. XVI, No. 43, the material following the close, though stable, brings the dominant into focus gradually. In the recapitulation Haydn omits much of this material. Though he retains the bifocal close, he weakens its effect by inserting a motif connecting it to the following bars.[23] This freedom reappears in the Piano Sonata H. XVI, No. 50. Although the transition ends on an inconclusive dominant, the secondary material confirms the new key in a way that sounds a bit perfunctory (bar 20):

Haydn: Piano Sonata, H. XVI, No. 50, first movement

by a bare melody implying the dominant key; explicit dominant harmonies do not appear until half a dozen bars later. Hence in retrospect the function of the bare melody is ambiguous, as Mozart blurs the distinction between transitional and secondary material.) A strange case is the slow movement of the Piano Sonata K. 576. The primary material concludes on a tonic cadence, and then is followed by a "transition" of three chromatic passing tones leading to a secondary area in the relative minor. In the recapitulation, the same tonic cadence is followed immediately by the secondary material in the tonic. Last, the most glaring oddity appears in a piece which, ironically, is often seen as epitomizing Mozartean symmetry and regularity: the popular C-Major Piano Sonata, K. 545. Here Mozart commences the "recapitulation" by stating the opening theme in the subdominant. He follows this with material leading to the bifocal close, after which the secondary material appears in the tonic. Hence the bifocal close acts as a "retransition" to the tonal return.

---

23   The relevance of the entire movement to this study is at all events uncertain. Georg Feder notes that the earliest ascertainable date is that of the first edition, 1783 (Preface to Haydn-Samtliche Klaviersonaten, Band III, München: G. Henle, 1972 [n.p.]). Christa Landon, however, dates the piece on stylistic grounds as "probably...from the early 1770s" (Preface to Haydn-Samtliche Klaviersonaten, Band Ia, Wien, 1966, p. XVII). If she is right, the bifocal close may be understood as an indicator of the lesser tonic-dominant polarity of the classical style prior to its full maturity.

Further, in the recapitulation Haydn alters not only the transition,

but the "monothematic" secondary material as well:

Here Haydn stretches the boundaries of the bifocal close to accommodate the maximum possible alteration of material. By preparing the tonic with a flatted-sixth chord and following it with what amounts to Romantic theme transformation, he gives the tonic return dramatic weight—weight which Mozart rarely attached to the bifocal close.[24]

In addition to his use of bifocal closes, Mozart's transitions minimize polarity in other ways as well. In the String Quartet K. 499, he begins with a tonic statement whose soft dynamic level and avoidance of full tonic triads makes it sound almost casual – hardly an expected posture for a polar tonal force:

Mozart: String Quartet, K. 499, first movement

---

[24]   Another example of unmodified bifocal close occurs in the slow movement of Haydn's String Quartet Op. 50, No. 6 – a minor-mode piece. More relevant is the major-mode finale of the same work, where Haydn's practice resembles Mozart's in K. 593, yet bears the characteristic stamp of his own monothematicism: the bifocal close is followed by a variant of the opening material now heard in (or rather on) the minor dominant, again preparing the ultimate goal of the major dominant. (In the recapitulation, the material in minor is simply left out.) In the second movement of the Piano Trio H. XV, No. 12, Haydn's practice is more conventional: his only modification is an expansion of the material of the bifocal close in the recapitulation. Last, in the second movement of the Piano Trio H. XV, No. 16, the primary material, in the minor, concludes on the tonic and is followed by a half-bar transition leading in the secondary area. Again, Haydn's monothematicism requires him to make an adjustment in the recapitulation. Since the secondary material is basically a major-mode version of the opening, he simply omits it.

The near-blandness sets up the following assertion of the relative minor, which thus sounds more powerful:

This momentary deflection acquires its very weight by the tentativeness of the opening material, and it obscures the larger issue of tonic-dominant conflict.[25]

In the String Quartet K. 464, Mozart's way of modulating is especially striking:

Mozart: String Quartet, K. 464, first movement

---

[25]   Mozart produces a similar result in a completely different way in the slow movement of the String Quartet K. 590. A modally flavored opening progression (tonic-supertonic) emphasizes lyricism at the expense of the larger tonic-dominant dramatic tension; and when the secondary area arrives, such tension is virtually absent.

The harmonic motion does not, so to speak, progress in a straight line (i.e., A-E-B, etc.), but is routed through C major, a (non-related) third away. Hence the large-scale root movement is not the typical Classic progression by fifths, but the Romantic one by thirds (A-C-E).[26] This gives us pause. The Classic progression produces steadily increasing long-range instability, since it moves away from home (the tonic) in a straight line. But a non-directional progression by thirds does not produce this effect of continually increasing distance from the tonic with increasing instability; and when the dominant does appear, it is not as a rival to the tonic but as just another point of harmonic repose. Hence when Mozart brings in the secondary material above (bar 37), its effect is not that of an opposing harmonic force, but of a *relaxation* of harmonic tension, in true Romantic fashion.[27]

A second factor revealing the extent of tonic-dominant polarity is the frequency of tonic chords in the dominant key area. Though heard of course in that context as subdominants, these chords are implicit references to the harmonic

---

26   Haydn, of course, also uses this type of root movement. But he nearly always employs it to articulate the beginning of a large section, such as the development (as in the "Military" Symphony), and only rarely to interrupt the motion from tonic to dominant in an exposition.

27   See Rosen's superb treatment of primary/secondary key relationships in Classicism vs. those in Romanticism in *The Classical Style*, pp. 382-84.

pole of the tonic. (This reference is sometimes made explicit through a tonicizing progression, as we shall soon see.) The more frequent – or prolonged – the reference to the tonic harmony, the less the polarity.

Here Haydn's and Mozart's practices are even more divergent. Indeed, in a few of his secondary areas, Haydn totally avoids subdominant chords (for example, in Symphonies Nos. 85, 92, 96, and 103). Most often the subdominant does occur several times, but only as a chord of short duration. The Symphony No. 88 furnishes a typical example:

Haydn: Symphony No. 88, first movement

In general, Haydn avoids sustained subdominant harmonies in his secondary areas. The simple straightforwardness, directness, forcefulness, and virility of his style depend on a sharp opposition between the two large-scale tonal forces of tonic and dominant. An intermingling of these two forces would compromise this opposition. It would effect a proximity of rival harmonic poles, a relaxation of the tension between thesis and antithesis, that is incompatible with the restlessness, the perpetual dynamic energy, of Haydn's music.

Sharply contrasting with Haydn's straightforward, black-and-white tonal world with all of its starkness, hardness, and tension, is the tonal world of Mozart – smoothly rounded and sensuous, more subtly tinted, and with a softer, richer harmonic ambiance. The opening of the "Linz" Symphony is an ideal case in point:

Mozart: Symphony No. 36, K. 425 ("Linz"), first movement

The immediate move to the subdominant foreshadows the subdominant emphasis of the primary material:

In the following tutti, Mozart revels in the rich, organ-like sonority of this plagal (tonic-subdominant) progression:

44

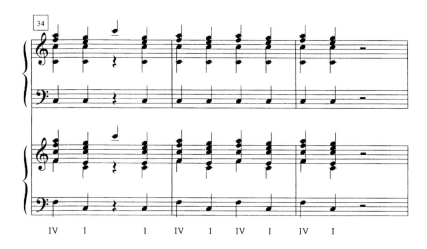

Such a fundamental bent toward the subdominant naturally continues into the secondary area, weakening the larger tonic-dominant polarity. After cadencing on the dominant – G – Mozart presents a theme, oddly, in E minor. But a turn to the local subdominant – C major – follows immediately. And on repetition, Mozart emphasizes the subdominant turn with a powerful tutti:

The subtlety and richness of the harmonic world of the "Linz" Symphony anticipate a similar tonal ambiance in a famous symphony written two decades later – Beethoven's "Pastoral." Again, the subdominant stress is a key element of the effect.[28]

The exposition of the "Prague" Symphony also opens with a theme heavily weighted toward the subdominant:[29]

---

[28]   Phillip Gossett, "Beethoven's Sixth Symphony: Sketches for the First Movement" (*Journal of the American Musicological Society*, 27, No. 2 [1974], pp. 248-84). A unique procedure occurs in the Piano Sonata K. 570, where Mozart's attraction to the subdominant results in a bold structural move: the actual secondary area material starts out in the subdominant and modulates to the dominant only after a half a dozen bars.

[29]   The subdominant weight is really a counterweight: by placing stress on the flat side of the tonic, Mozart counterbalances the approaching move to the dominant. This explains Rosen's observation: "The opening of a work by Mozart is always solidly based, no matter how ambiguous and disturbing its expressive significance, while the most unassuming first measures of a quartet by Haydn are far more unstable, more immediately charged with a dynamic movement away from the tonic" (*The Classical Style*, p. 186).

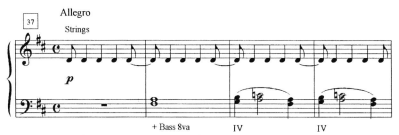

+ Bass 8va   IV   IV

Mozart: Symphony No. 38, K. 504 ("Prague"), first movement

IV

Again, the subdominant emphasis continues into the secondary area, weakening the tonal polarity. In this instance, Mozart calls attention to the subdominant with a chord progression that suggests an explicit reference to the home key – a tonic intrusion into the dominant sphere:

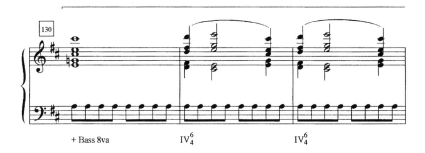

+ Bass 8va   IV$_4^6$ IV$_4^6$

47

IV$^6_4$

Even in so massive a structure as the "Prague" Symphony,[30] Mozart crosses back and forth between the two harmonic poles with ease.

The most extraordinary instance of all occurs in the "Haffner" Symphony. All through the transition, Mozart seems unusually reluctant to make a clean break with the tonic. At measure 48, however, a modulation begins – apparently in earnest:

Mozart: Symphony No. 35, K. 385 ("Haffner"), first movement

---

30   See the excellent analysis in Rosen's *Sonata Forms*, pp. 194-217.

But when the secondary key area arrives, the music continues to oscillate:

The dominant harmony then continues to alternate, now with a minor tonic replacing the major. After a powerful unison passage in the dominant, closing material duly appears. Yet even as it concludes the exposition, the material still seems partially anchored to the tonic:

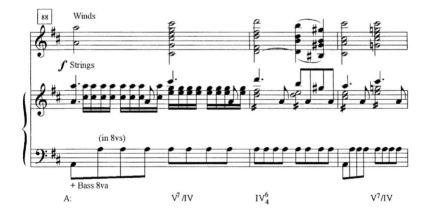

In the "Haffner" Symphony as in no other work, the shadow of the tonic still hangs over the entire dominant area. Two tonal poles operating simultaneously create a harmonic ambivalence that makes the piece unique. More important, the fact that Mozart generally avoids a neat compartmentalization of his tonic and dominant poles opens up a harmonic world that is richer than Haydn's. This all-encompassing tonal vision provides of course a perfect musical context for the complex web of human interactions, entanglements, and intrigues that is the very stuff of which his operas are made.

Mozart's stress on the subdominant is especially strong in his piano concerti. This genre requires separate consideration. Showing as it does vestiges of the Baroque ritornello principle, which emphasizes melodic recurrence rather than overall harmonic structure, it does not display the same capacity for large-scale tonic-dominant polarity as does the symphony or string quartet. Hence this seemingly Mozartean trait may to some extent be inherent in the genre itself.

Nevertheless, the subdominant emphasis in these pieces is striking:

Mozart: Piano Concerto No. 17, K. 453, first movement

The immediate subdominant reference at the opening of K. 453 functions as a counterweight similar to that in the opening of the "Prague" Symphony. And its effect is conspicuous: it occurs in the course of a melody that is especially rich in affective content, revealing Mozart in his best operatic form. He is playfully witty, as he presents a rhythmic ambiguity in the very opening bar (does the measure represent an upbeat or a downbeat?). Yet he hints at an underlying wistfulness and resignation, particularly in the expressive sigh at bar four, where the F-natural intensifies the subdominant feeling. The implications are far-reaching. Charles Rosen rightly regards this movement as one of Mozart's military allegros.[31] Yet when compared with the first movement of the Piano Concerto K. 467, for example, its fanfare seems muted, its high spirits subdued. The very different orchestration is of course a factor: in the later piece trumpets and drums create a festive brilliance here totally absent. But even more revealing is the different harmonic contour of its opening. Instead of the confident, marchlike tune of K. 467 with its straightforward tonic-dominant harmonies, Mozart presents here his more characteristic, softer, plagal ambiance. The harmony of these opening eight bars casts a wistful shadow over the whole movement.

Such harmonic premonitions are not found in his earlier Piano Concerto K. 414. In its opening ritornello, Mozart generally avoids subdominant references; he saves them for the closing material. Here, in order to emphasize the subdominant, he adopts the opposite procedure of K. 453. Instead of using the chords to support a beautiful melody, he writes them into purely conventional material. In the absence of melodic interest, the harmonic element naturally comes into the foreground. It is a gentle fluctuation between twin poles, the local tonic

---

31   Albeit an unusually "graceful and colorful" one (*The Classical Style*, p. 221).

and the long-range tonic (the local subdominant). The entering strings (bar 137) suffuse the music with the soft warmth and richness of Mozart's tonal world – a childlike, fairy-tale world where no matter how far one travels harmonically, home is never far away:

Mozart: Piano Concerto No. 12, K. 414, first movement

52

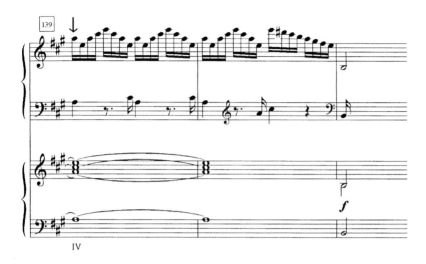

IV

Other piano concerti may be cited. In K. 456 the subdominant reference is emphatic rather than gentle (bars 181-83). In K. 459 the tonicizing progression, dominant of the subdominant to subdominant (or leading tone of the subdominant to subdominant), is heard no fewer than eight times (bars 165-72), and then eight more times as the passage is repeated (bars 175-81). And in K. 488, Mozart concludes the exposition with a variant of the opening ritornello (bar 137): a beautifully piercing melody whose subdominant stress helps to create the melting warmth that permeates the entire piece.

The extent of tonic-dominant polarity is greater in Haydn than in Mozart. This conclusion is congruent with other stylistic characteristics of the composers that have a bearing on the issue. Is it not plausible that Haydn's music has greater harmonic freedom because his harmonic poles are further apart, giving him more tonal space in which to move without threatening ultimate tonal stability? And in view of his frequent monothematicism (not to mention the motivic nature of the themes themselves), may not much of the interest of his music lie in a greater tension and opposition of basic harmonic forces? Conversely, a function of Mozart's contrasting lyrical themes may be to provide for the basic need of opposition and contrast, which his harmonic forces – being less strongly polarized – supply only to a lesser degree.

Chapter Two

Tonal Deflections

The operatic character of the Classical style is especially obvious in the phenomena known as tonal deflections. These passages occur most often in the dominant area, between secondary and closing material. While appearing within this larger context of tonal stability, they nevertheless depart – often suddenly – from the prevailing key center and set up temporary competing centers (the local flatted mediant and flatted submediant are common choices). The unexpected twist, the sudden turn of events, implied by such deflections is closely bound up with the dramatic nature of the High Classical style. An early and striking example occurs in Mozart's *Idomeneo* (1781). In the celebrated quartet from Act III, Idamante sings of his desire to seek death alone and his father, Idomeneo, cries out in despair, while Ilia swears her love to him and jealous Electra calls for revenge. The vehicle for these powerful dramatic sentiments is none other than sonata style. The piece is in E-flat: hence the secondary key area is in B-flat. But at the words "Ah il cor mi si divide" ("Ah, my heart is breaking") Mozart shifts darkly to B-flat minor. Then, as all four characters sing "Più fiera sorte, pena maggiore nessun provò" ("No one ever suffered a harsher fate or greater punishment"), the music takes a sudden and breathtaking turn to D-flat (the local flatted mediant). When the same words recur in the recapitulation within a context of E-flat, Mozart repeats the passage not in the expected G-flat but down a third from the tonic in C-flat (the flatted submediant), thereby preserving even at the repetition the element of harmonic surprise.

This operatic emphasis on dramatic events, on unexpected harmonic turns, was carried over into the instrumental repertoire. It is immediately recognized as a trademark of the Classical style:

Mozart: Piano Concerto No. 17, K. 453, first movement

In Mozart's Piano Concerto K. 453, the function of the deflection is architectural as well as dramatic. Having incorporated this harmonic gesture into the opening ritornello, Mozart then uses it to articulate the development as well:

56

Having hinted earlier at the richness of possibilities implicit in a dominant-to-flatted-submediant progression, Mozart now explores them in a remarkably expansive development whose chromaticism is particularly far-ranging.

The function of the deflection is more complex in the Symphony No. 39 finale. The movement begins with a square, regular tune:

Mozart: Symphony No. 39, K. 543, fourth movement

Such regular melodic construction carries the inherent danger of monotony, especially in a monothematic movement such as this one. Mozart solves the problem by inserting a harmonic twist that is completely unexpected (bar 52):

The deflection has another function as well. The initial occurrence of the secondary material (at bar 42, identical to bar 48 above) sounds a bit tentative, with its harmonization in first inversion rather than root position. The stability of B-flat as a larger tonal center is then challenged by Mozart: he temporarily abandons the key, only to make a marvelously smooth, rapid transition back to it (bars 62-66), conferring upon it greater strength than it originally possessed.

The Symphony No. 40 presents a more complex picture. The initial modulation is dramatic, as the relative major bursts upon the scene as a bold new gesture. In comparison, the secondary material (bar 44) sounds on arrival rather reticent. But as the phrase is repeated the plot thickens:

Mozart: Symphony No. 40, K. 550, first movement

The deflection at bar 58 opens a door on yet another harmonic vista, the key of A-flat. But at bar 63 Mozart makes his decisive move: with the diminished-seventh chord the music breaks free, and the relative major reasserts itself triumphantly. Once again, the deflection has effectively strengthened the secondary key.

The most striking of Mozart's deflections appears in the "Jupiter" Symphony. Though the dominant is well prepared by a strong modulation, the initial secondary material sounds less like a full-blown theme than a tentative phrase:

Mozart: Symphony No. 41, K. 551 ("Jupiter"), first movement

Its fragmented melodic line and its first-inversion harmonization are, in one sense, ill-suited to material announcing the arrival of a large-scale tonal area. Once more, Mozart issues a challenge – this time one of overwhelming power (bar 81):

The impact of this deflection results from several factors: the preceding dominant preparation and suspenseful pause, the sudden tutti, the pedal point (whose stability produces a tremendous expansiveness), and the modal mixture (C major/minor), which yields an expressive intensity. But again the return is to a tonic now stronger than ever before (bar 89). In a sense, the entire deflection is a large-scale cadence reaffirming the key of G: iv (bar 81)-IV (bar 83)-I (bar 87)-V (bar 88)-I (bar 89). Yet if it is a local event when viewed from this perspective, it nevertheless has far-reaching implications. For Mozart uses similar dramatic strokes in the second and fourth movements (at bars 19 and 127). Surely this points to the uniqueness of the "Jupiter" – an enormous tonal mass in C major, melodically rather undistinguished in its outer movements, and stamped with three brief, stormy intrusions of the minor mode. It is precisely the neutral quality of much of the melodic material that renders these harmonic strokes so effective.

Even more typically Mozartean than a deflection is a related device: the modal mixture. The "Prague" Symphony furnishes a lovely example:

+ Bass 8va

A : I
Mozart: Symphony No. 38, K. 504 ("Prague"), first movement

Such major-minor mixtures may be viewed essentially as modified deflections: deflections which progress only as far as the parallel minor. Yet they yield a distinctive effect – the intensified melodic expressiveness that is a salient feature of Mozart's style. Such modal shifts are quintessentially Mozartean: their emotional ambivalence, implicit pathos, and expressive subtlety give his music that particular affective quality so unmistakable, yet so difficult to capture in words.[32] The impulse is again operatic: here the conflicting emotions of a leading character – perhaps a betrayed lover who nevertheless remains faithful – are given

---

32   Mozart's fascinating expressive qualities are given a remarkably articulate treatment in W. J. Turner's *Mozart: The Man and His Works* (London: Methuen and Co., 1965, reprint), pp. 301-10. Turner's discussion is descriptive rather than analytical.

purely instrumental expression.[33]

Another type of modal shift occurs when the transition sets up the minor dominant, and then is followed by secondary material in the major. Such instances are infrequent, but striking. The slow movement of the G-major Quartet, K. 387, furnishes a rare example:

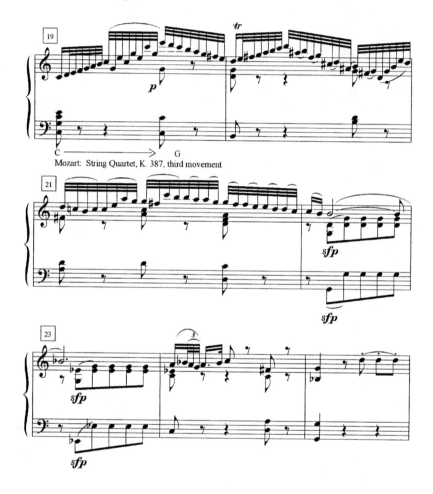

Mozart: String Quartet, K. 387, third movement

---

33   Other instances of this type of modal shift, with its extraordinary subtlety of expression, are found in the piano concerti K. 467 (slow movement, bar 12) and K. 503 (first movement, bar 17).

66

At the appearance of the secondary material (bar 31), the placement of the third in the bass intensifies the modal change. Nevertheless, the overall result of this approach to the dominant is a more relaxed tonal ambiance at the secondary key area, as the relative tension of the minor yields to the greater stability of the major. The device reappears in the slow movement of the "Jupiter" Symphony, where it helps to create the stormy intrusion mentioned earlier:

+ Bass 8va

F ——————> C

Mozart: Symphony No. 41, K. 551 ("Jupiter"), second movement

68

This suggests a further possibility of sonata style: the presentation of the initial secondary material in the minor dominant. Here again, an operatic precedent is found in *Idomeneo*. In Act I, Idomeneo, caught in a storm at sea, vows to sacrifice to Neptune the first person he meets upon landing, if the god will grant him safety to harbor. When he arrives his first encounter is with his own son, Idamante, and he flees from him in despair. In the following aria, "Il padre adorato," Idamante expresses his grief at his father's strange behavior. Again, sonata style is the perfect vehicle for the expression of powerful emotions: at the secondary area Idamante sings, "M'uccide il dolor" ("The grief is killing me") in the minor dominant. And this unusual procedure also occurs several times in Mozart's instrumental music. One instance occurs in the slow movement of the String Quintet K. 593:

Mozart: String Quintet, K. 593, second movement

In a sense, this represents a variant of his procedure in the "Jupiter." However, the passage beginning at bar 16 seems to have just enough melodic profile to mark it as the secondary area material. The recapitulation confirms this:

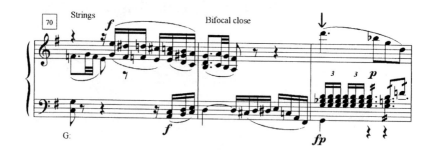

Even the bifocal close can be pressed into service, illustrating once more the flexibility of sonata style. In the exposition, Mozart's ultimate tonal goal is D major. Rather than preparing it with a transition, he employs the bifocal close, followed by a stable passage in the parallel minor, and then a short chain of sequences (bars 22-25) leading to a cadence in the new key: subdominant, to dominant, and eventually to tonic. In a real sense, then, the passage in D minor and the chain of sequences share a function usually given to the transition: they prepare for the long-range tonal goal.

In the slow movement of the G-minor Quintet, K. 516, a soaring melody in the dominant (bar 27) is first prepared by a dark, mid-range passage in the minor dominant. The pulsating accompaniment figure intensifies the drama of the unexpected minor:

Mozart: String Quintet, K. 516, third movement

Mozart is recalling here the turbulence of the first movement. The Neapolitan (bars 24-25) intensifies the expressiveness created by the minor mode. Finally, both of the secondary area themes highlight the critical third (bars 18 and 27); at the modal shift the D-natural soars nearly two octaves above the accompaniment. The change could hardly be more dramatic.

Several such appearances of secondary material occur in the piano concerti. In this most operatic of instrumental forms, where the piano serves as the leading protagonist in the drama, Mozart's use of the modal mixture is especially effective: it creates both dramatic impact and formal expansion. In K. 482, the piano has the powerful declamatory material – recalling the duel in Act I of *Don Giovanni* with its sudden darkening of mood:

Eb —> Bb :
Mozart: Piano Concerto No. 22, K. 482, first movement

76

The passage serves a structural function as well. Bars 131-33 prolong and expand the preceding four bars, and are in turn expanded in the bars that follow, while bars 139-46 contain two patterns of pianistic figuration, each heard twice. Hence Mozart delays the arrival of the major material. When it finally appears (bar 152), it provides a long-awaited, welcome contrast to the earlier dramatic outburst and protracted minor harmonies; its childlike naiveté and charm are doubly gratifying for their delayed arrival.

In K. 467, the initial minor appearance of the secondary material is foreshadowed by a modal shift in the opening ritornello:

Mozart: Piano Concerto No. 21, K. 467, first movement

IV

The deflection itself does not stretch the dimensions of the movement quite as far as that in K. 482, but its function is the same:

80

Again, Mozart uses prolongation and repetition of internal material to delay the arrival of the major dominant (bar 128). Once more, after the tension of the minor, the diatonic simplicity of the innocuous melody is doubly welcome.[34]

The operatic impulse underlying the piano concerto genre provides the perfect milieu for this type of modal mixture. In both concerti it is the piano, the leading protagonist, that suddenly breaks loose with the minor material. By using this arresting tonal gesture, Mozart brings the solo instrument even more fully into the spotlight.

The expressive subtlety of a modal mixture is a striking facet of Mozart's style. Such subtlety is foreign to Haydn. When he uses a modal mixture, it is to different purpose:

---

[34]   Mozart's practice is similar in the Piano Concerto K. 595 (bar 100), while in K. 537 (bar 128) he compromises with initial secondary material that fluctuates between major and minor.

Haydn: Symphony No. 84, first movement

In the Symphony No. 84 the sudden intrusion of the minor tonic (bar 81), however dramatic, merely serves to facilitate the move to the flatted submediant, the temporary tonal goal. Haydn is using the modal shift as a harmonic pivot.[35] At the same time, the function of the deflection, like that in Mozart's "Jupiter," is cadential: it leads from the flatted submediant (bar 85) through a tonic six-four chord (bar 94) and ultimately to a dominant-seventh-to-tonic progression.

This cadential function is more explicit in his String Quartet Op. 50, No. 6. While still in the transition, Haydn gives a clear indication of the secondary key

---

[35]   Mozart occasionally proceeds this way (as in the finale from the Symphony No. 39, cited earlier [bar 50]). But more often, he goes only as far as the parallel minor.

with two bars of stable tonicizing reiterations (bars 30-32):

Haydn: String Quartet, Op. 50, No. 6, first movement

He then uses the deflection, disruptive though it is, to settle fully into the new key:

85

Both here and in the symphony, the large-scale cadence strengthens the dominant, and ultimately increases the tonic-dominant polarity.

Indeed, Haydn was gradually moving towards Mozart's practice in Mozart's last symphonic trilogy: strengthening a tentative-sounding secondary area by following it with a deflection. The Symphony No. 91, written in the same year (1788) as Mozart's final three, marks Haydn's arrival at this practice. The transition begins with the usual tutti, but its harmony is completely diatonic:

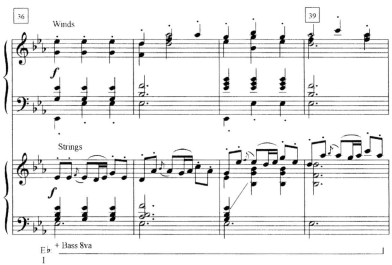

Haydn: Symphony No. 91, first movement

In particular, the two pedal points (bars 36-39 and 49-52) function as tonic anchors, resulting in one of Haydn's less dramatic transitions. Hence the arrival of the secondary key area sounds rather tentative, especially for Haydn:

The motif is familiar as that which opened the exposition (now with an added counter-melody). But, as in the Mozart symphonies, the long-range "staying power" of the new key needs to be proven. If it is to assume plausibility as a larger tonal center, it must show sufficient resilience to absorb some chromatic shocks and still stand. The deflection supplies these shocks:

89

Further, its graceful melody at bar 88 (more engaging than the actual thematic motif at bar 57) provides the passage with an added weight and interest which are more characteristic of Haydn's deflections than Mozart's. Forceful tonicizing reiterations are required to reaffirm the tonal supremacy of B-flat. They are underscored by a concluding tonic pedal and triplet flourish:

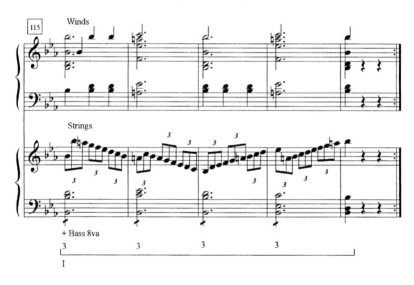

The melodic interest of the deflection is crucial to Haydn's procedure. Since the primary and secondary area material are nearly identical, the new melody supplies a necessary variety.[36]

---

[36]   A similar instance occurs in the String Quartet Op. 50, No. 2, where the opening theme also serves as the closing material (though slightly altered). The appearance of the graceful new melody (bars 66-75) is particularly welcome.

Haydn's remarkable ability to use deflections to supply precisely the needed dramatic function reaches a peak in the String Quartet Op. 76, No. 2 ("Quinten"). The piece opens with the stark descending fifths that lend the quartet its nickname:

Haydn: String Quartet, Op. 76, No. 2, first movement

The initial pedal point and the repetition of the first three bars (an octave higher) create a static plateau. The listener is now primed for the kinetic energy of a transition. Instead, Haydn proceeds directly to the secondary area material:

Though more animated rhythmically, the passage is tonally stable. Hence the listener tends to hear it as the opening of the secondary key area. But it trails off rather loosely:

93

Now Haydn unleashes his master stroke:

The highly charged tension of this stormy, minor-mode deflection makes it the dramatic high point in the exposition. Further, the beautiful sequence (starting at bar 36) creates such expressive richness as to blur the distinction between the deflection and the "thematic" material.

Melodically significant in a different way is the deflection of the "Emperor" Quartet, Op. 76, No. 3. Haydn, again using a shift to the minor as a harmonic pivot, incorporates the opening melodic material into the deflection in a particularly conspicuous way (starting at bar 32):

Haydn: String Quartet, Op. 76, No. 3 ("Emperor"), first movement

95

The brief pause (bar 32) and the subsequent contrapuntal entries combine to give the deflection a real formal autonomy.

In the Symphony No. 102, Haydn's formal play takes him a step further. A powerful transition prepares the dominant, F. But when the new key arrives, the listener receives a shock:

Haydn: Symphony No. 102, first movement

The deflection actually inaugurates the secondary area.

This shows how thoroughly a deflection may be incorporated into the larger structure of a movement. Haydn does this in a different way in his String Quartet Op. 54, No. 3. The piece is in E major; hence the secondary area is in B. The deflection – to G – occurs at the very end of the exposition:

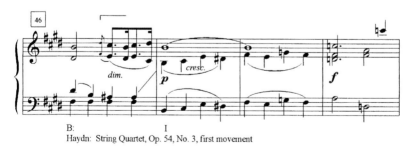

Haydn: String Quartet, Op. 54, No. 3, first movement

The placement of the deflection gives it a dual function. As heard initially (during the first statement of the exposition) the deflection raises some doubts about the stability of B major. With the return of the E-major opening things fall into place: the augmented-sixth chord at bar 53 is confirmed (retroactively) as part of a large-scale augmented-sixth-to-dominant-to-tonic progression. But the second time around, the deflection foreshadows the opening of the development, which launches out in the key of G:

Still more impressive is Haydn's creative inventiveness in the String Quartet Op. 64, No. 2. The opening sounds a bit unsettled:

Haydn: String Quartet, Op. 64, No. 2, first movement

Adding to the restlessness of the minor mode are the tonal ambiguity of the opening solo and the deceptive cadence. With the arrival of the secondary key the music assumes relative stability:

But after half a dozen bars, the stability is shattered:

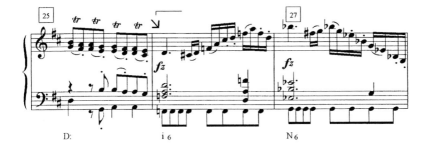

99

Haydn's genius here lies in his economy of procedure. Basically the deflected passage is a simple modal shift, in which the Neapolitan (bar 27) serves to launch a chromatically ascending scale (in the bass: G-A♭-A-B♭-B-C♯-D). The seemingly arbitrary chromaticism of bars 28-30, then, occurs within a secure tonal framework of G-D. It is the virtual halt of rhythmic activity at bars 28-29 that obscures this framework, so that the passage sounds more harmonically remote than it really is. But it is in the development that Haydn's inventiveness reaches its peak. He begins, significantly, with a chromatically ascending progression in the bass:

This leads to material from the deflection, now inverted:

He then alters the following deflection material, yielding an extraordinary breadth and expansiveness:

Hence the deflection is integral to Haydn's overall conception of the movement, since its material provides an expressive weight that results in an almost autonomous development section.

As is by now clear, the term "deflection" is in one sense a misnomer. Though accurate in terms of larger tonal goals, its connotation of a passage standing apart from, perhaps even unnecessary to, the essential structure – a sort of musical parenthesis – is false. The weight of these passages belies such a notion. Haydn and Mozart focus the listener's attention on them in a number of ways, including the use of sudden tuttis or new melodic material. Their importance to the overall structure is frequently borne out by their appearance as elements within large-scale cadences, or by their recurrence in the development. Most remarkable of all is the capacity of a deflection to serve as a kind of harmonic litmus test for the initial secondary material; once passed, this test leaves the secondary key stronger and more stable than before.

Mozart's music contains an added and more subtle dimension: that of modal shifts. The same dramatic instinct that enables him to depict such fine gradations of human emotion in his operas is at work in his instrumental music. The result is an expressive poignancy – subtle, yet intense – which is one of the most affecting qualities of his style. These shifts occur most often within the secondary area. In a few instances, they occur between transitional and secondary material. Their effect here is to lower the level of tension at the appearance of the dominant. Finally, in several cases they result from the choice of the minor dominant as the initial secondary key. This prolongs some of the harmonic tension of the transition over into the relatively stable secondary area. These cases particularly evidence the principle underlying the use of all types of deflections: flexibility of formal procedure in the service of continuous dramatic interest.

Chapter Three

Structural Junctures

In the Classical style harmony and form are of course closely related. The formal divisions of exposition, development and recapitulation derive their meanings from the large-scale harmonic motions occurring within them: in the exposition a progression from tonic to dominant, in the development continuous modulation eventually leading back to the dominant, and in the recapitulation a reaffirmation of the tonic.

Especially critical to the unfolding drama of a sonata-style movement is the kind of harmonic motion which occurs at the junctures between these divisions. The first is the exposition-development break. Here, four different kinds of harmonic movement are possible. At one extreme is juxtaposition – an immediate and dramatic confrontation between two keys. It occurs when the final chord of the exposition, i.e., the dominant (or in minor-mode movements the relative major), is followed *directly* by the tonic chord *of a new key,* with the new tonality sustained for a credible period (for the purposes of this study, a minimum of four measures). A far more frequent practice is of course modulation. Naturally, this may involve various degrees of suddenness: sometimes it is abrupt, while in other movements it begins before the double bar and hence is much smoother.[37] But invariably the music leaves the dominant – or contains

---

37   Beginning the modulation before the double bar creates an ambivalence. The actual point of articulation is blurred (especially if the rhythm is continuous at the juncture [i.e., no rests are involved]). And yet if the listener concentrates on the larger structure, he does hear the development being ushered in gradually by a change of key. Broadly speaking, then, its appearance is highlighted by an event. Haydn and Mozart proceed this way in about one fifth of their movements. Among these are the first movements of Haydn's Symphonies Nos. 94 and 96, his String Quartets Op. 33, No. 3, Op. 64, No. 5, and Op. 76, No. 2, and Mozart's Symphony No. 36, String Quartets K. 421 and 465, and String Quintets K. 515 and 516. The procedure does not seem related to any other harmonic or formal features.

chromaticism signaling the *beginning* of such a departure – either shortly before or immediately after the start of the development (for the purposes of this study, at a point no later than two bars after its beginning). A related phenomenon is a change of mode: a simple shift from major to minor (again within two bars). Finally, the other end of this spectrum is represented by tonal continuity: the dominant key is sustained, with no hint of an approaching modulation, for a reasonable period (again, for our purposes, a minimum of two bars).

A schematic presentation highlights the different compositional priorities of the two composers.[38] Movements not listed use modulation.

Haydn: Symphonies

Juxtaposition		Modal Change		Continuity	
Symphony	Movement	Symphony	Movement	Symphony	Movement
97	First (V-III♭)*	83	Fourth	84	First
98	First (V-III)	86	First	84	Fourth
98	Fourth (V-VII♭)	89	First	95	First
100	First (V-III♭)	90	Fourth	100	Fourth
		99	Second	101	First
				104	Fourth

*Opening theme reappears in new key

---

[38] This listing of course excludes movements without developments.

Haydn: String Quartets

Juxtaposition		Modal Change		Continuity	
Quartet	*Movement*	*Quartet*	*Movement*	*Quartet*	*Movement*
Op. 33 No. 1	Third (V-iii)*	Op. 76 No. 1	Fourth	Op. 42	First
Op. 33 No. 6	First (V-III♭)			Op. 50 No. 2	First
Op. 50 No. 6	Second (III-I♭)*			Op. 50 No. 5	First
Op. 54 No. 3	First (V-III♭)*			Op. 64 No. 3	Fourth
Op. 76 No. 4	First (V-iii)*			Op. 64 No. 6	First
				Op. 74 No. 2	Fourth
				Op. 76 No. 1	First
				Op. 76 No. 2	Fourth
				Op. 76 No. 3	Fourth
				Op. 77 No. 1	Fourth

*Opening theme reappears in new key

Haydn: Piano Trios

Juxtaposition		Modal Change		Continuity	
Trio	*Movement*	*Trio*	*Movement*	*Trio*	*Movement*
[none]		H. XV No. 6	First	H. XV No. 12	Second
		H. XV No. 8	First	H. XV No. 15	First
		H. XV No. 16	First	H. XV No. 22	First

107

Juxtaposition		Modal Change		Continuity	
Trio	*Movement*	*Trio*	*Movement*	*Trio*	*Movement*
[none]		H. XV No. 20	First	[none]	
		H. XV No. 24	First		

Haydn: Piano Sonatas

Juxtaposition		Modal Change		Continuity	
Sonata	*Movement*	*Sonata*	*Movement*	*Sonata*	*Movement*
[none]		[none]		H. XVI No. 43	First
				H. XVI No. 49	First

All other Haydn movements with developments use modulation.

Haydn: Statistics

- Total movements above, including those using modulation.. 157
- Total movements using key juxtaposition, modal change, continuity, or modulation........................ 149**
  - Movements using key juxtaposition.............. 9 (6%)
  - Movements using modal change.................... 11 (7%)
  - Movements using continuity.......................... 21 (14%)
  - Movements using modulation......................... 107 (72%)

** Eight movements incorporate structural elisions (the slow movements of Symphonies Nos. 87 and 98; the finales of Nos. 93 and 95; the slow movements of String Quartets Op. 71, No. 2, Op. 76, No. 5, and Op. 77, No. 1; and the finale of Piano Trio H. XV, No. 10).

Mozart: Symphonies

Juxtaposition		Modal Change		Continuity	
Symphony	*Movement*	*Symphony*	*Movement*	*Symphony*	*Movement*
[none]		[none]		35	First
				35	Second
				36	Second
				36	Fourth
				38	First
				38	Third
				41	Fourth

Mozart: String Quartets

Juxtaposition		Modal Change		Continuity	
Quartet	*Movement*	*Quartet*	*Movement*	*Quartet*	*Movement*
K. 590	Fourth (V-VI♭)	K. 458	Fourth	K. 387	First
		K. 464	First	K. 428	First
		K. 499	First	K. 458	First
		K. 589	First	K. 499	Fourth

Mozart: Quintets

Juxtaposition		Modal Change		Continuity	
Quintet	*Movement*	*Quintet*	*Movement*	*Quintet*	*Movement*
[none]		[none]		K. 406	First
				K. 407	First

Mozart: Piano Sonatas

Juxtaposition		Modal Change		Continuity	
Sonata	*Movement*	*Sonata*	*Movement*	*Sonata*	*Movement*
[none]		K. 533 & 494	First		
		K. 545	First	K. 547a	First
		K. 576	First		

All other Mozart movements with developments use modulation.

- Total movements above, including those using
  modulation.. 56
- Total movements using key juxtaposition,
  modal change, continuity, or modulation............. 54**
  - Movements using key juxtaposition.............. 1 (2%)
  - Movements using modal change.................. 7 (13%)
  - Movements using continuity........................ 13 (24%)
  - Movements using modulation....................... 33 (61%)

** Two movements incorporate structural elisions (slow movements of String Quartet K. 499 and String Quintet K. 593).

All of the above movements are in standard sonata form, that is, they involve an exposition, a development, and a recapitulation. Two categories of works have necessarily been omitted: the piano concerto, in which the precise point of the exposition-development break is ambiguous, and also (for the same reason) movements containing structural elisions.

Mozart's more frequent use of modal change at the break is in keeping with his greater fondness for modal mixtures in general. But the most striking difference between the two composers is Haydn's more frequent use of key juxtaposition. (Mozart's sole example, the finale of the String Quartet K. 590, occurs in one of his most Haydnesque movements.[39] A borderline case is the slow movement of the same quartet.) Though proportionately small, these instances have a significance greater than statistics suggest: they show Haydn's awareness that dramatic surprise need not be limited to local events but may also articulate the larger structure. In several instances – those marked with an asterisk – he further highlights the break by presenting, in the new key, the opening theme, either literally or altered.[40] Hence the effect is that of a new beginning. In the

---

[39]   Notice the opening theme, the gypsy-rondolike turns of phrase (bars 16-20), the continual stopping and starting showing an interest in local play (bars 38-50), and the delayed arrival of the dominant. Hence the sudden jolt at the beginning of the development, resulting from the key juxtaposition, is in keeping with the style of the piece.

[40]   Mozart sometimes operates similarly (e.g., the Symphony No. 40). But since he never incorporates key juxtaposition into the proceedings, the effect is not nearly as dramatic.

Symphony No. 97 the effect is further intensified by the fanfare-like quality of the opening motif:

Haydn: Symphony No. 97, first movement, opening of exposition

A more subtle approach appears in the slow movement of the String Quartet Op. 33, No. 1, where Haydn alters the melody at the beginning of the development. Yet within the context of the movement the effect is nevertheless marked – partly because of the dark change to the minor mode:

Haydn: String Quartet, Op. 33, No. 1, third movement, opening of exposition

End of exposition, beginning of development
A:

F ♯

112

More suspenseful is the break in the Symphony No. 98. At the opening of the development the unexpected piano, the suddenly bare texture, and the ominous hints of minor (bar 134) inject an air of mystery into the music:

Haydn: Symphony No. 98, first movement, end of exposition

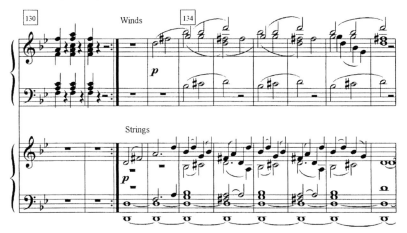

Beginning of development

Haydn's more dramatic articulations at this juncture are also reflected in his movements which use modulations. As might be expected, they are more sudden than Mozart's. An example is the finale of the D-minor String Quartet, Op. 42:

113

Haydn: String Quartet, Op. 42, fourth movement, end of exposition

G:
Beginning of development

In the Piano Sonata H. XVI, No. 41, Haydn opens the development by repeating the last two bars of closing material. To make certain that the listener does not miss the formal break, however, he not only changes dynamics, register, and spacing, but also makes a remote harmonic leap:

Haydn: Piano Sonata, H. XVI, No 41, first movement, end of exposition

114

Beginning of development

Mozart's modulations, on the other hand, are better described as compressed. Like Haydn, he often covers much harmonic ground within a few measures, but he is more consistent in supplying a chord or a harmonic progression that functions as a pivot. In the finale of the String Quintet K. 593, the pivotal passage ends on a triad (bar 102) which then doubles as the first member of a deceptive chord progression:

Mozart: String Quintet, K. 593, fourth movement, end of exposition

115

Beginning of development

Like Haydn in his Symphony No. 97, Mozart launches the development with an arresting dramatic gesture; unlike Haydn, he nevertheless preserves harmonic continuity.

Even when he opens the development with the primary area material, Mozart deliberately softens the effect of a new beginning. In the Clarinet Quintet, K. 581, he once again begins the development with a modulation. But a shift to the parallel minor eases the listener into the new key. The move is swift, yet gentle:

Mozart: Clarinet Quintet, K. 581, first movement, end of exposition

116

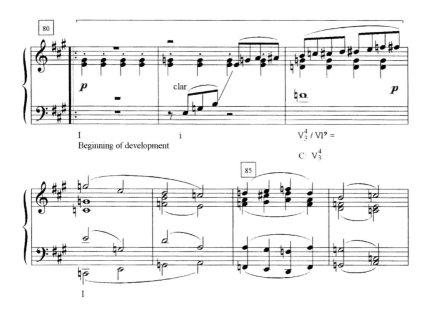

In the Symphony No. 40, the return of the primary material is blended with a descending scale in the woodwinds – a smooth master stroke that deftly underplays the return of the opening melody:

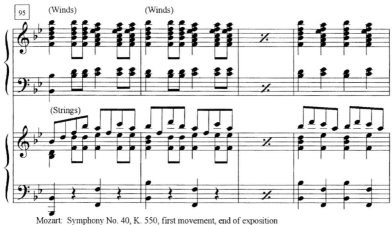

Mozart: Symphony No. 40, K. 550, first movement, end of exposition

117

Primary material

Beginning of development

+ Bass 8va

In the "Dissonant" Quartet, K. 465, Mozart's procedure has large-scale harmonic significance. At the opening of the exposition, a tonic pedal creates a conspicuously stable effect (especially coming after the chromatic twists and turns of the introduction):

118

Mozart: String Quartet, K. 465, first movement, beginning of exposition

When this material reappears (slightly altered) at the beginning of the development, the pedal point is on a dissonant B-flat. The instability immediately betrays the transitory character of what is to follow:

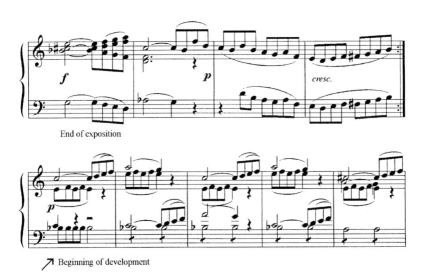

The instability is resolved, of course, only by the return of the tonic at the recapitulation. Yet at a still broader level, the question raised by the dissonant B-flat is not answered until the coda (specifically, at bar 235):

119

Not only is the long-range harmonic emphasis unique to Mozart, but the more nuanced articulation of the exposition-development juncture is far removed from the dramatic juxtapositions of sections found in Haydn. The seeming paradox is that nowhere is Mozart's concern for continuity more evident than in his treatment of these formal breaks.

A total of ten Haydn and Mozart movements contain structural elisions: the final cadence of the exposition overlaps the beginning of the development. An example is the slow movement of Haydn's Symphony No. 87:

Haydn: Symphony No. 87, second movement, end of exposition

121

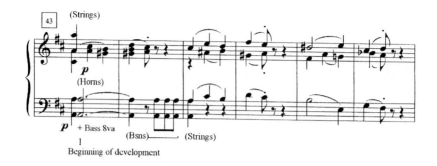

Beginning of development

Indeed, most of the examples are found in slow movements, where the lesser emphasis on large-scale structure (in favor of local expressive details) results in an occasional slurring over of important formal junctures. But in several instances the elision is related to a critical event occurring later in the movement. In Haydn's Symphony No. 98 the elision precipitates a sudden powerful modulation, which seems disorienting:

Haydn: Symphony No. 98, second movement, end of exposition, beginning of development

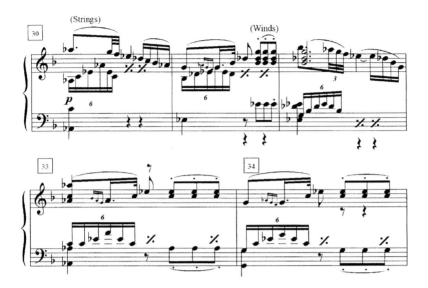

One becomes aware that a juncture has been crossed, but only gradually and in retrospect. The full meaning of the sudden modulation does not become clear until after measure 30, where the remote key and subsequent sequence (measures 33-34) signal the emerging development. This oblique articulation of the larger structure recurs at the next formal juncture, but in an entirely different way:

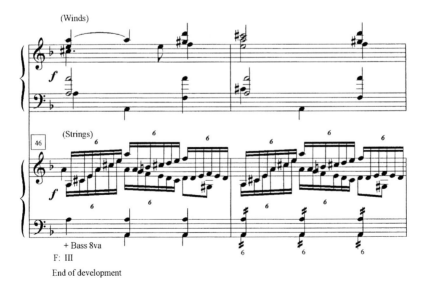

123

Vc. solo
Beginning of recapitulation

Haydn underplays the return by using a non-dominant retransition (one which is centered on the mediant). The usual tension-resolution pattern of a dominant-tonic progression is conspicuously absent. (The effect of the return is further diminished by the cello obbligato, which carries some of the rhythmic momentum of the development over into the recapitulation.) Hence, both the elision and the non-dominant retransition imply an underlying looseness of structural articulation.

The finale of the Symphony No. 93 represents another case where Haydn opens the development with an elision (around bar 135) and concludes it with a non-dominant retransition (here on the leading tone, starting around bar 154). The same applies to the finale of the Symphony No. 95 where the retransition is on the mediant. Here the elision is part of the formal fluidity of the entire movement. There is no definite break between transitional, secondary, and closing material; rather, the music runs on in a largely continuous stream of eighth-notes for 45 bars (from bar 33 until the start of the development at bar 78). Both here and in the finale of No. 93, the developments are exceptionally short. Their brevity, their squarely symmetrical themes, and their non-dominant retransitions, all point to the strong influence of the rondo in these movements.

The other main structural juncture is that between the development and the recapitulation.[41] The nature of the retransition is of course critical here. Two specific factors are involved. As the development runs its course, a descending sequence occasionally effects a lowering of tension (Mozart is especially fond of this practice). The other device, even more telling, is the dominant pedal point. Both are involved in Mozart's String Quintet K. 515:

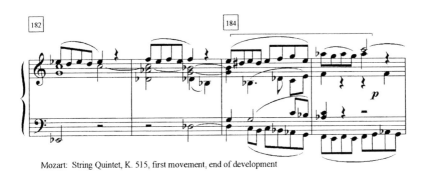

Mozart: String Quintet, K. 515, first movement, end of development

---

41   Much less important is the juncture between the recapitulation and the coda. Codas appear in only one-fifth of the movements at hand. Among these, only a few have the structural and expressive weight of the famous coda in the finale of Mozart's "Jupiter." A number, however, do give a strong sense of formal autonomy, including those in Haydn's Symphonies Nos. 92 and 97, his String Quartet Op. 76, No. 2, the finale of Op. 74, No. 2, and his Piano Trio H. XV, No. 16. Unique are the codas of Haydn's Symphony No. 103 and Mozart's String Quintet K. 593, both of which are delineated by the return of the slow introduction. Both Haydn and Mozart totally avoid key juxtaposition in articulating their codas. Although Mozart, interestingly, begins his codas with a modulation slightly more often than Haydn, he never uses a sudden, dramatic change of key, as does Haydn in the "Oxford" Symphony and in the Piano Trio H. XV, No. 16.
      Haydn and Mozart occasionally begin the recapitulation with exposition material originally heard in (or at least *on*) the secondary key, now transposed to the tonic. Such instances are few: the finales of Haydn's Symphony No. 87 and String Quartet Op. 54, No. 3, the finale of Mozart's String Quartet K. 387, and the slow movement of his Piano Concerto K. 467. A unique case is the first movement of Mozart's famous Piano Sonata K. 545, where the thematic "recapitulation" begins in the subdominant.

Beginning of Recapitulation

The retransition commences at bar 184. Although the sequence begins to dissipate tension immediately, it is the lengthy pedal on the dominant that basically prepares the return. A more famous example is the "Jupiter" Symphony. Its descending sequence is unusually chromatic:

+ Bass 8va

Mozart: Symphony No. 41, K. 551 ("Jupiter"), first movement, end of development

127

This anticipates a similar passage in the finale – at the adjustment at bar 233, where the chromaticism is even denser. In both K. 515 and the "Jupiter," the impressive proportions of the dominant preparation again show Mozart's hand. Indeed, in over a quarter of his movements (as opposed to approximately a tenth of Haydn's), Mozart first signals the impending return of the tonic by sounding the dominant at least a dozen bars before the recapitulation. Although other chords usually follow, a pedal point on the dominant invariably precedes the final resolution to the tonic.

Mozart's preference for longer retransitions is related to another characteristic of his style: his retransitions are invariably centered on the dominant.[42] The sole instance of a non-dominant retransition, in the slow movement of the String Quartet K. 590, is the exception that proves the rule:

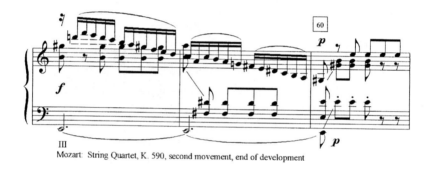

Mozart: String Quartet, K. 590, second movement, end of development

---

[42] Dominant retransitions are defined here as those which make any use of the dominant whatsoever; non-dominant retransitions are those which totally avoid it. In exceptionally rare instances, such as Haydn's Piano Trio H. XV, No. 30, a diminished chord on the leading tone (vii°) substitutes for the dominant. In such instances the harmonic progression at the juncture involves tension and resolution very similar to a dominant-tonic progression; these may therefore be viewed as dominant retransitions. A unique instance appears in Haydn's String Quartet Op. 74, No. 2. Here Haydn straddles the line between a dominant and a non-dominant retransition: eight bars of pedal point on the major mediant are followed by a dramatic silence, then a unison progression consisting of a submediant, the critical leading tone, and the tonic return.

C: I
Beginning of recapitulation

ii

The device occurs in the context of a style which effectively anticipates Schubert: the tonic-supertonic progression of the primary material, the absence of harmonic tension at the arrival of the dominant, and particularly the articulation of the development, where the modulation by a third creates a harmonic ambiance which sounds distinctly Romantic:

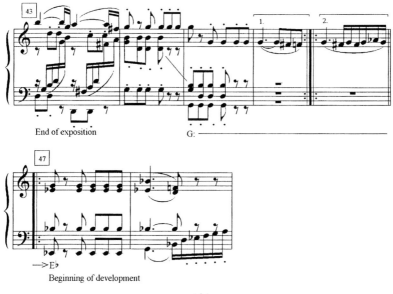

End of exposition

G:

—>Eb
Beginning of development

131

Haydn, on the other hand, uses the device in over a dozen movements.[43] Interestingly, his non-dominant retransitions are often longer than those on the dominant.[44] In his Symphony No. 85 ("La Reine"), the tonic return is preceded by no less than twenty-one bars of the major mediant:

Haydn: Symphony No. 85, ("Le Reine"), first movement, end of development

---

[43]   The implied tonality of these retransitions is removed from the immediate orbit of the dominant; common harmonic centers are the mediant and submediant, or (most often) a mixture of both. Besides the finales of Symphonies Nos. 93 and 95 and the slow movement of No. 98, they occur in the following: first movements of Symphonies Nos. 85, 90 and 94, and of String Quartets Op. 54, No. 3, Op. 64, Nos. 3 and 6, and Op. 76, No. 3, second movements of the Symphony No. 99, and of Piano Trios H. XV, Nos. 12 and 13, third movements of the String Quartet Op. 33, No. 1, and of the Piano Trio H. XV, No. 27, and the finale of the Symphony No. 104. Another difference in Mozart's and Haydn's procedures involves the use of a fermata just before the recapitulation – a device found more often in Haydn than Mozart. It seems more congruent with the return of the tonic as a local event, rather than as one which involves the resolution of long-range tension.

[44]   See his Symphony No. 90 (bars 138-52), the second movement of his Piano Trio H. XV, No. 13 (bars 138-53), and the finale of No. 27 (bars 149-62).

Beginning of recapitulation

Haydn's penchant for non-dominant retransitions can be explained by his very different concept of harmonic movement. Basic to Mozart's style is a feeling for long-range harmonic tension and resolution.[45] It is this larger harmonic sense – involving long-delayed resolutions of tensions raised earlier – which (among other gifts) accounts for his preeminence as an operatic composer. Indeed, for Mozart the establishment of the dominant in an exposition corresponds to the creation of a major dramatic conflict in the course of an operatic plot. Since the dramatic events that follow are at a lower level of tension than those in a movement of Haydn, the basic tonic-dominant conflict remains clearly in view. (Recall for example Mozart's smoother treatment of his exposition-development breaks, where he avoids sudden modulations.) At the development-recapitulation juncture, then, Mozart, with long-range continuity foremost in his mind, picks up the conflict where it left off. When he writes a dominant retransition – sometimes of considerable length – he is making reference to a harmonic problem raised earlier. With the return of the tonic, the conflict is resolved.

Haydn is more concerned with local harmonic events. The retransition of "La Reine," for all its twenty-one bars of length, is, harmonically speaking, a highly dramatized, exceptionally prolonged local event. The dramatic gesture of

---

45   Charles Rosen, *The Classical Style*, pp. 79, 185-86.

large-scale tension-resolution intrinsic to a dominant-tonic progression is absent.

Yet if Haydn's retransitions do not carry the larger harmonic implications of Mozart's, he shows a more intense formal awareness in his treatment of the exposition-development juncture. To be sure, his conception allows for a more flexible treatment than Mozart's, varying from dramatic key juxtapositions to elisions which eliminate any formal break whatsoever. In the final analysis, however, Haydn, chiefly by reason of his sudden modulations, is more consistently concerned with dramatic, decisive articulation of his developments than Mozart. The strong formal awareness which this implies is critical to Haydn's style. Just as Haydn's greater tonic-dominant polarity allows him more harmonic freedom to move without endangering essential tonal stability, his more powerful sectional articulations give his larger formal procedures a more distinct outline – enabling him to take more liberties at a local level without impairing the lucidity of the overall structure.

Chapter Four

Development Procedures

The grace, ease, and facility so closely identified with Mozart appear not only in his effortless stream of melodic invention, but also in a less likely stylistic dimension: his development procedures. Of all possible developmental devices – thematic inversion, variation or combination, unexpected modulation, etc. – Mozart seized upon the sequence as his quintessential element. Hence in one sense his developments write themselves; their basic impetus is supplied by a stock device that is as fundamental to tonality as are scales and triads.

In what is perhaps his best-known symphony, No. 40, Mozart writes an opening in which he gives the restless agitation of the accompaniment a Classical counterpoise by his smoothly flowing melody with its sequential outline. In the development Mozart immediately explores the latent harmonic potential of this sequence. (Numbered brackets designate units within larger sequences.)

+ Bass 8va

Mozart: Symphony No. 40, K. 550, first movement

136

A sequential descent of a dozen measures comes to a temporary halt on E (measure 112-17), only to sink downward for sixteen more bars before reaching a further point of rest:

137

Though the sudden change of texture at bar 139 signals a new section, the effect of the articulation is lessened by the continuity of the motif. At the retransition, sequential continuity again prevails, but now over a dominant pedal. The last member of a woodwind sequence leads directly into a beautifully elided return: the re-introduction of the main tune requires an extra measure to disentangle itself from the retransition:

[Dominant prolonged to]———>

In the finale of the "Linz" Symphony, a single continuous sequence consumes most of the development:

Mozart: Symphony No. 36, K. 425, ("Linz"), fourth movement

Mozart's partiality towards sequences was to find ample endorsement in the course of the nineteenth century. With the generation of Schumann and Mendelssohn, they appear in increasingly large blocks – sometimes with near-fatal consequences. In Schumann's Piano Quintet Op. 44 (published in 1843), he presents a block of material thirty-four bars long (bars 128-61). The material itself is already packed with sequences; Schumann then repeats the entire block transposed down, initially to a minor third, and then (after a brief harmonic adjustment) to a major second (bars 167-202). Thus Schumann's development is essentially divided into two even halves. While the expressive power of the music

140

at a local level is indisputable, the large-scale effect is curiously static.

This stasis results largely from a fundamental change in musical language that had first become evident two decades earlier as an early portent of the dissolution of the Classical style: the loss of harmonic dissonance at the level of the larger structure. In the eighteenth century this structural dissonance had given sonata-style movements a large-scale dynamic tension. In major-mode movements it had appeared in the familiar guise of tonic-dominant polarity. Yet it was equally strong in pieces in minor keys. Indeed, the most dramatic example of its potential for tension and conflict is the opening movement of Beethoven's Fifth Symphony: the tonal opposition between the worlds of C minor and E-flat major lies at the very heart of the work, creating an almost cosmic struggle.

This structural harmonic dissonance is crucial to the continuous tension of a sonata-style movement. Particularly in the case of Mozart, the larger tension that results is not confined to the exposition, but remains suspended, as it were, throughout the development; Mozart's blocks of sequences are heard against a larger background of tonal conflict. Since the listener expects a resolution, the sequences seem propelled by a powerful underlying dramatic impulse. By contrast, the Schumann piece projects little large-scale tension, as its drama is confined to local events. The underlying de-emphasis of tonic-dominant polarity is reflected in the tentative, hesitating quality of the secondary area material. Hence a major structural element is largely absent, and Schumann's development is left without supporting harmonic girders. In the absence of large-scale harmonic tension, the mechanical quality of Schumann's sequences becomes all too apparent. The inevitable result is stasis.

This is not so much an indictment of Schumann's style as a reflection of the changes in tonal language that appeared during the second quarter of the century. Viewed as a three-part essay in open-ended thematicism, the movement is beautifully effective.

Mozart's sequences are not always derived from his expositions: they occasionally make use of new material. In the String Quartet K. 458, the development commences with an entirely new periodic melody in the dominant. Its regularity nearly obscures the exposition-development juncture:

Mozart: String Quartet, K. 458, first movement, end of exposition   Beginning of development

142

This material is followed by a chain of sequences (beginning at bar 106) that might be construed as rhythmically related to secondary area material:

But melodically it is brand new, and Mozart uses it as a vehicle for twenty-one bars of further development.

Similarly fresh, though conventional, ideas appear in the String Quartet K. 428. The sequences are on a larger and more irregular scale (compare measures 79-82 with 83-88), but do not inhibit the basic flow of conventional material unrelated to the exposition:

143

Mozart: String Quartet, K. 428, first movement

The grace note in the pattern hints at an interesting connection probably intended by Mozart: its execution as a triplet suggests that it is derived from the opening of the second group:

Mozart's passion for sequences fashioned out of the simplest materials emerges most conspicuously in his piano concerti, as for example in No. 21, K. 467:

Mozart: Piano Concerto No. 21, K. 467, first movement

147

The sequences here are combined with a closely related device: circular root movement. This involves a bass-line progression of three or more steps employing the same interval (generally a fifth, occasionally a third). Such progressions – here a typical circle of descending fifths, E-A-D-G-C-F – supply a sturdy harmonic framework for Mozart's brilliantly virtuosic piano writing. The challenging passagework in this movement is doubtless what moved Leopold Mozart to describe this concerto as "astonishingly difficult."[46]

46   *The Letters of Mozart and His Family*, trans. and ed. by Emily Anderson (London: Macmillan, 1938, III), p. 1333, n. 3.

In the Piano Concerto K. 491 (measures 309-46), an enormous block of filler presents two such sequences (G-C-F-etc.), separated by a scant half dozen bars of tonal stability (measures 323-29). The second sequence (starting at 330) is dovetailed to yet a third block of sequences, now in descending thirds, consuming the entire development right up to the retransition:

Mozart: Piano Concerto No. 24, K. 491, first movement

151

In K. 595, a series of descending thirds (measures 178-83 – F-D-B) blurs over the beginning of the development, and leaves the piano rather unceremoniously in the remote key of B minor:

Mozart: Piano Concerto No. 27, K. 595, first movement

Once again the tonal stability is short-lived, as this opening solo itself turns out to be the first member of yet another sequence. Two more are to follow. The first consists of the usual circle of fifths (bars 210-18). The second is more complex. It incorporates two successive plagal progressions ($E^\flat$-$B^\flat$ and f-c), creating a relaxed, introspective quality in keeping with the autumnal mood of this, Mozart's last piano concerto. The violins, playing a variant of the opening melody in stretto, create a rich, expansive effect, tinged with the poignancy of the minor mode:

153

Although Mozart's use of the sequence is a constant element in his developments, two factors vary widely: the number of themes treated sequentially, and the amount of repetition of a given theme within a sequential block. The development of the finale of the Symphony No. 39 is similar to that of the "Linz" Symphony. A single thematic unit is repeated five times:

Mozart: Symphony No. 39, K. 543, fourth movement

155

Greater thematic economy cannot be imagined. Just the opposite is Mozart's procedure in the opening movement of the "Prague" Symphony, where each of four blocks of development is supplied with its own motif (marked A-D). The result is a contrapuntal texture of increasing complexity and richness:

Mozart: Symphony No. 38, K. 504 ("Prague"), first movement

156

IV

Yet the wealth of melody is not quite as extravagant as it might seem. Three of the four themes share a similar harmonic outline (A and B suggest the same harmonic profile presented in the minor mode by C). Hence the rich potential for thematic combination.

Despite its more numerous themes and sequential blocks, the development of the "Prague" Symphony is similar in effect to that of the "Linz" finale, since its four groups of sequences flow smoothly into each other; in both movements the momentum carries the listener through to the recapitulation. Hence there emerges a concept of the archetypal Mozart development: a self-perpetuating flow of sound, in which sequences predominate over tonal plateaus, and in which sudden dramatic events are avoided.

This concept of development as continuity, often based on conventional material, contrasts sharply with Haydn's more variegated procedures and greater inventiveness:

Haydn: Symphony No. 89, first movement

Here the initial continuity is broken simply by the fermata (bar 62). But the main cause of the sectionalization is Haydn's greater use of stable harmonic plateaus. Measures 63-74 form a twelve-bar block of pure diatonic E-flat major, a simple melodic repetition of the opening material. The sequential pattern that follows ushers in a second harmonic plateau, derived from transitional material:

160

+ Bass 8va

The sequential pattern continues, coming to an end at bar 88:

At bar 93 a third plateau arrives: fifteen bars in D minor, consisting largely of secondary and closing material. Hence by the end of the development, primary, transitional, secondary, and closing material have appeared, and (interestingly enough) *in their original order*.[47] This illustrates anew a well-known point about sonata style: its crucial element is harmony, rather than melody. Haydn is not afraid to repeat the overall melodic pattern of the exposition because the arrival of each new tonal center is a fresh event that gives the movement continual interest. The new tonal relationships are striking: the primary material is in E-flat (bar 63), the transition begins in F minor (bar 77), and the secondary and closing material appear in D minor (bars 93 and 98). The shift to the minor mode helps provide the tension and harmonic instability vital to a development.

In the finale of the String Quartet Op. 76, No. 3, Haydn uses a pedal point on A-flat to break up the flow:

---

[47] Order preservation within developments was not unique to Haydn. The opening movements of Mozart's G-minor Quintet and Beethoven's Fifth Symphony are two celebrated examples. It is the profusion of thematic material that sets the Haydn movement apart.

Haydn: String Quartet, Op. 76, No. 3 ("Emperor"), fourth movement

The material itself is familiar (bars 99-102 are drawn from the closing area). It is the sudden turn of harmonic events that gives the passage its impact. Not satisfied with a simple disruption of forward motion, Haydn then intensifies this disruption with two dominant-tonic reiterations that emphatically assert the new tonal center.[48]

As these pieces make clear, the discontinuities within Haydn's developments in no way preclude a highly organic construction. It is precisely his plateaus that permit extensive restatements of stable exposition material. The contrast with Mozart is strong. Even discounting the genre of the piano concerto (where Mozart's emphasis on arpeggios and passage-work rather than thematic development arises from his interest in pianistic virtuosity), Haydn is more consistent and thorough in exploiting the possibilities inherent in his themes.

This highly organic conception of development is related to another critical dimension of Haydn's music: the intrinsic nature of his material. Compared to Mozart's beautiful cantabile melodies, Haydn's themes often have the deliberately neutral quality of tonal building blocks. Hence they lend themselves quite naturally to use as elements in formal construction.[49] In his String Quartet Op. 33, No. 3, this neutral quality applies even to the harmonic implications of the opening theme. Or rather its lack of any such implications:

Allegro moderato

C: 1^6

Haydn: String Quartet, Op. 33, No. 3 ("The Bird"), first movement

---

[48]   In several piano trios (H. XV, Nos. 14 and 28, and the finale of 22) Haydn's use of such tonal plateaus affects the notation of the music – the plateaus are delineated by an actual change in key signature.

[49]   See the very brief but excellent discussion of Haydn-Mozart differences in H. C. Robbins Landon's *Haydn Symphonies* (London: British Broadcasting Corporation, 1966), pp. 10-11.

For two and a half bars the tune sits on the fifth degree of the scale. This elemental simplicity allows Haydn to dress up the theme with a new harmonic interpretation at the beginning of the development,

and yet another at the recapitulation:

His thoroughness and ingenuity in exploiting his material are evident almost immediately. Seven bars into the development, he not only presents the theme altered and in halved note values, but combines it with a variant of secondary area material (originally appearing in measure 30):

In the tonal plateau that follows, the larger harmonic movement is of course at a halt. Yet organic development continues. The section is built mostly upon closing material:

Even its details are derived from the exposition. Compare bars 80-84 with bars 32-33:

and 41-43:

More diminution of the opening material leads to a fermata and a new section, where a one-bar introduction at bar 98 (taken from the very opening of the exposition) brings in another variant of the secondary material (see measure 30 above):

A four-bar passage (measures 103-6), drawn again from the secondary area (bars 37-40), concludes this most organic of developments.

The String Quartet Op. 71, No. 1, shows that Haydn could create organic, tightly constructed developments with even the most innocuous of materials:

Haydn: String Quartet, Op. 71, No. 1, first movement

The opening motif (itself drawn from the opening theme) is accompanied by simple scale figures derived from the secondary area:

Measures 39-43 (cf. mm. 75-76)

Measures 44-48 (cf. mm. 75-76)

And the material that launches the following sequence (starting at bar 84) is drawn from the primary area,

and the closing area:

Perhaps Haydn's supreme example of organic construction within a sectional framework occurs in his String Quartet Op. 77, No. 1. The development begins with a sequence based on the opening theme. Haydn then writes a string of apparently modulating sequences based on seemingly conventional material (bar 69):

Haydn: String Quartet, Op. 77, No.. 1, first movement

173

174

But the passage really goes nowhere tonally: it is a "closed section" in E minor. And the material is not filler, but derives from the transition:

The passage beginning at measure 82, taken from the secondary area, leads to a new section based on the opening theme. This section cadences and is followed by yet another, delineated by an unexpected modulation (bars 104-5) and based again on the secondary area. Here the bass line (A-D-G) reveals a device more typical of Mozart – a circle of fifths. But the interruption of momentum (at bar 109) disrupts the sequential regularity:

Haydn's resourcefulness as a musical craftsman naturally brings to mind his great successor. Beethoven similarly creates highly organic developments in which he often breaks the regularity of his sequences. The crucial difference lies, of course, in his expansion of proportions. In the "Eroica" Symphony, the enormous development consumes 245 bars. Commencing softly upon a harmonic plateau in C major, Beethoven then builds to the first of numerous tuttis, in D

176

minor (bar 186). The section that follows is based largely on a fragment from the opening theme, heard in the bass. The section is then repeated sequentially in G minor (bar 198). But this time the sequence is expanded: the last four bars of the passage are repeated in F minor, and the last bar of this F-minor segment in turn is treated sequentially. All of this settles down to a quiet tonal plateau in the relaxing subdominant, A-flat (bar 220), repeating the material heard earlier in C. However, Beethoven soon builds tension again, this time with contrapuntal sequences climaxing on a powerful diminished chord, whose syncopated reiterations inhibit the sense of forward motion. At this point Beethoven intensifies the effect of his formal expansion by a dramatic distension – the music reaches a point of immobility:

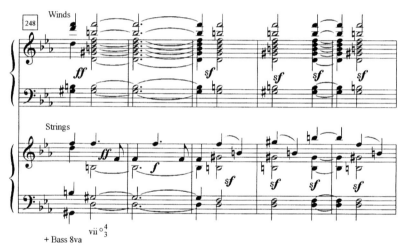

Beethoven: Symphony No. 3, Op. 55 ("Eroica"), first movement

177

And just one bar later, when this rhythmic pattern is repeated on a dominant seventh chord, an eruption of the tympani confirms that Beethoven is doing something which transcends mere sequential continuity. After a harmonic detour to the Neapolitan (here supplied with the famous jarring dissonance of an added seventh), the music settles at last into E minor. What follows is in one sense simply another harmonic plateau. But in a larger sense, it is the ultimate in formal expansion: a beautiful new melody appears in the oboe – periodic, perfectly stable, and unrelated to anything heard earlier.[50] The listener almost forgets that he is still in a development section. Beethoven's expansion of structure has affected the very nature of his development: more than ever before, it is fully capable of standing alone as a full-blown musical gesture, in the same way as the exposition and recapitulation.

One might attribute Haydn's strongly organic concept of the development to the string quartet genre itself; the potential for contrapuntal thematic combinations in a medium involving four players would be an open invitation to such development. But this would not do justice to the composer. For Haydn's other chamber and solo works, among them the Piano Sonatas H. XVI, Nos. 34, 43, 49 and the Piano Trio H. XV, No. 17, also provide striking evidence of organic developments. One example will suffice: the Piano Sonata H. XVI, No. 41. In this piece, tonal plateaus and thematic derivation fairly abound. Haydn launches his development with closing material drawn from the exposition, employed in a colorful key juxtaposition:

Haydn: Piano Sonata, H. XVI, No. 41, first movement

50   The curious derivation offered by Charles Rosen in *The Classical Style* (p. 393) ignores the critical role played by rhythm.

He then presents the opening theme – and in so doing, a nine-bar plateau on E-flat. Using a motif from the transition (compare bars 68-71 with 24-27),

he begins a modulation to G minor, where he presents a tonal plateau,

which is based on another transitional passage (compare bars 80-83 with 38-41):

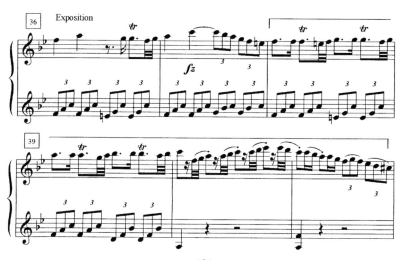

He then leads into the retransition via ascending chromatic scales, again drawn from the transition.

Examples from Haydn's output are nearly endless. They all show his consummate skill in manipulating expository material to form a tightly knit, strongly organic development.[51]

Another device that appealed particularly to Haydn is the false recapitulation. The term generally refers to a return of the opening material in the tonic, but a return which is used as a springboard for further development, rather than marking the beginning of the actual recapitulation. Here it will be used in a wider sense to designate any stable restatement of the opening material (regardless of key) which occurs around, or after, the halfway point in the development – thus having "plausibility" as a recapitulation. This will yield a broader perspective on the element of ambiguity within the drama of a sonata-style movement.

Drama is indeed key to false recapitulation. Its effectiveness depends on a surrounding context of musical events tightly controlled by a larger tension. The listener must *expect* a true return in order for the play on expectations to be effective. For this reason, the device fell into disuse during the nineteenth century, with its declining emphasis on large-scale dramatic structure. Two further stylistic

---

[51] There remains the category of slow-movement development sections. With Haydn these are proportionately shorter, and with both Haydn and Mozart less contrapuntal in texture, than those in fast movements (for example Haydn's String Quartets Op. 33, No. 1 [third movement], Op. 50, No. 6 [second movement], Op. 71, No. 2 [second movement] and the second movements of Symphonies Nos. 83, 86, 87 and 99; Mozart's Quintets K. 406 and 593, and Symphonies Nos. 35, 36, 38, 40 and 41 [all second movements]). As might be expected, the slow tempo is more conducive to an emphasis on expressive melodic and harmonic details: for example, those found in two strikingly similar passages, the second movements of Haydn's Symphony No. 98, bars 15-25, and of Mozart's "Jupiter" Symphony, bars 28-39. Other examples of this emphasis are found in the slow movements of Haydn's Symphonies Nos. 83 and 99, and of Mozart's No. 38.

tendencies, closely interrelated, also contributed to its disappearance. One was the increasing predilection for tentative-sounding openings. This appears as early as Beethoven's Ninth Symphony: the faint opening rustle in the strings has the effect of blurring the transition from silence to sound. (This device was to become a stylistic stamp of Anton Bruckner.) Such an opening is hardly conducive to a false recapitulation – it lacks sufficient articulation. Related to this is the Romantic tendency to give greater weight to the secondary area of an exposition than to the primary (e.g., the first movements of Schubert's "Unfinished," Brahms's Second, and Tschaikovsky's "Pathétique" symphonies). Again, this would weaken the effect of a false recapitulation, whose dramatic significance depends on the emphatic nature of its material.

In the eighteenth century, however, its element of unexpected drama was ideally suited to the operatic quality of the Classical style. It appealed more strongly to Haydn (who used it twelve times) than to Mozart (who used it only once). This is not surprising, since the device combines four elements already inherent in Haydn's style: his concept of developments as derived organically from exposition material, his penchant for harmonic plateaus, his interest in formal manipulation, and his love of local surprise.

The last feature has particularly strong implications. The degree of ambiguity in a false return lies somewhere between two extremes: the total deception of a perfectly literal return in the tonic, and the deliberate equivocation of a substantially altered one in a foreign key. Thus Haydn commands a wide range of possibilities in playing upon the expectations of his listeners.

Complicating the issue, however, is Haydn's frequent practice of writing actual recapitulations which themselves differ from the opening in details of melody, harmony, or orchestration. Nevertheless, Haydn is able to create a meaningful play on expectations with his false returns. The all-important factor is the presence of the tonic. When it returns, it is ordinarily a sign that the recapitulation has begun, so that slight alterations are insignificant. But when the tonic is absent, a void is sensed; such deviations carry more weight, and confirm the listener's suspicion that something is amiss.

And in most cases something is indeed amiss. Haydn's false recapitulations usually occur in keys other than the tonic. His most salient alterations of opening material are found in his symphonic works. In chamber

183

music, where he is writing for a smaller audience – one that is perhaps more sensitive to formal details – he is more subtle. The Piano Trio H. XV, No. 11, shows him at his most artful:

Haydn: Piano Trio, H. XV, No. 11, first movement

Establishing F: V

184

At bar 119 he writes a brief dominant preparation; Haydn, the master of formal play, is preceding his false recapitulation with an emphatic "false retransition." To deceive his listeners further, he then writes a false return that parallels the first dozen measures of the exposition, with only the slightest changes in ornamentation (bar 121 in the piano part), spacing (bar 121 in the violin part), and octave placement (bars 123-24 in the violin part).

An entirely different kind of subtlety appears in the finale of his String Quartet Op. 64, No. 3. Again Haydn sets up the false return with a "false retransition." This time, he hints at the presence of an irregularity by commencing his adjustment unusually soon – after just four bars of "recapitulation:"

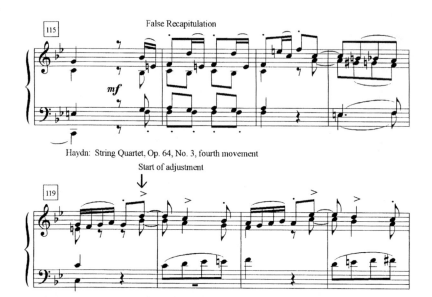

False Recapitulation

Haydn: String Quartet, Op. 64, No. 3, fourth movement

Start of adjustment

The listener is left to fend for himself.[52]

A slight change of timbre is the only alteration in the String Quartet Op. 71, No. 3, as Haydn simply shifts from a three-part to a four-part harmonic texture by filling in the viola line.[53] In the Piano Trio H. XV, No. 14, the change is more obvious. The accompanying violin and cello of the opening are now silent, and the false return is left to the piano alone:

---

[52]   Haydn uses a similar procedure in the finale of the Piano Trio H. XV, No. 22.

[53]   In the String Quartet Op. 64, No. 6, the change involves harmony, but is nevertheless very slight.

186

Haydn: Piano Trio, H. XV, No. 14, first movement

187

This is one of Haydn's most effective false recapitulations. The silence of the strings is conspicuous; as if to allay temporarily the suspicions of his listeners, Haydn extends the false recapitulation so that it parallels the exposition for a full fifteen measures. The play on expectations is thoroughly Haydnesque.

A unique procedure appears in the String Quartet Op. 33, No. 4. The entire piece shows Haydn in a particularly capricious mood, beginning with its whimsical opening:

Haydn: String Quartet, Op. 33, No. 4, first movement

Half a dozen bars into the development there begins a seemingly endless string of sequential progressions, which is a bit unusual for Haydn. The plateau which finally arrives at bar 48 turns out to last for a mere two measures. It is a false return. Naturally, the listener then prepares for another sequential chain. What follows (at bar 51) throws him completely off guard:

By now this is the last event that he has been primed to expect – the true recapitulation.[54]

An enigmatic case is the String Quartet Op. 64, No. 5 ("Lark"). At measure 105 in the development, there is a literal repetition of a full eleven bars of the opening material, and in the tonic key:

Haydn: String Quartet, Op. 64, No. 5 ("Lark"), first movement

And the following twenty-six bars sound more like an adjustment passage than a continuation of the development. Far from disturbing the stability of the tonic, they end up reinforcing it:

---

[54] In the finale of the String Quartet Op. 76, No. 6, Haydn replaces formal play with rhythmic play; he precedes the "false retransition" (bar 87) with a passage whose displaced accents disorient the listener rhythmically.

Hence the earlier passage might be viewed as the beginning of the true recapitulation. If so, the next statement of the primary key area would be seen as a merely gratuitous repetition of the opening material – especially since its clockwork accompaniment causes it to be absorbed into the flow of the music:

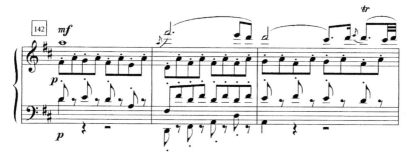

Nevertheless, the all-determining factor appears in the measures that follow (153-68). These bars correspond unmistakably with the original transition, with the material now adjusted to remain in the tonic. Hence the last example is best viewed as the true recapitulation, and the passage beginning at 105 is indeed a false recapitulation.

In his orchestral music Haydn avoids such sophisticated formal plays with false returns. Perhaps he felt that they would be wasted on the less refined sensibilities of his large symphonic audiences. This does not imply any lack of interest in local surprise; he simply makes his effects with broader strokes. In the Symphony No. 96, seven bars of chordal reiterations imply a resolution to the submediant. After a dramatic pause, Haydn presents a false recapitulation, but in the unexpected subdominant. The effect recalls the non-dominant retransition of the first movement of "La Reine" (see pp. 132-33). Haydn is ostensibly taking special pains to prepare a move to a particular key, but when the move finally occurs it is to an entirely unexpected key:

Haydn: Symphony No. 96 ("Miracle"), first movement

193

In the Symphony No. 102, Haydn launches the exposition with a powerful tutti, followed by a quiet restatement of the material in the strings, with flute doubling:

Haydn: Symphony No. 102, first movement

This allows for a remarkable stroke at the false recapitulation. After twenty-three bars of forceful contrapuntal drive, Haydn inserts a dramatic silence, and then the false return. It is given to the solo flute, an evident reference to the second statement of the theme at the opening. The sudden quiet creates a striking effect:

The most atypical of Haydn's false returns occurs in his Symphony No. 91. The opening theme is unusually gentle:

+ Bass 8va
Haydn: Symphony No. 91, first movement

195

After such an undramatic opening, it is only natural for Haydn to gloss over the false recapitulation. Yet this false return contains a feature which, ironically, causes it to deceive only his more sophisticated listeners: it is in the tonic. As if in compensation for this deception, Haydn underplays the return. He omits any kind of preparation, placing it within a context of continuous flow:

Mozart uses the false recapitulation only once in his entire mature repertoire, in the "Jupiter" Symphony.[55] The most telling evidence of a conceptual distinction between the two composers is simply that Mozart's practice here is similar to Haydn's atypical procedure in his Symphony No. 91: he places the false return in a context of continuous flow. Further, the variants which appear show that Mozart is attenuating the effect of the device. Having opened the movement with an arresting tutti,

Mozart: Symphony No. 41, K. 551 ("Jupiter"), first movement

he then writes a quiet false recapitulation in the subdominant – the most common key for a false return, and one that is considerably less "deceptive" than the tonic of Haydn's symphony:

---

55   Discounting the well-known Piano Sonata K. 545, where the thematic "recapitulation" begins before the return of the tonic.

197

198

Mozart's hesitancy to write a false return that is genuinely deceptive is further evidenced by his radical changes in dynamics and orchestration. No listener can mistake for long the subdued, incidental reference to the primary area theme for the bold, arresting gesture that opens the piece.

All of this is consistent with the stylistic differences between the two composers. Mozart shares little of Haydn's fondness for local surprise, organic construction, or tonal plateaus, characteristics well suited to false recapitulations. He prefers to avoid the device and maintain his characteristically smooth sequential flow and continuity.

Haydn's and Mozart's development procedures imply a basic conceptual difference between the two composers. Mozart's greater use of sequences (sometimes constructed from pure filler) and his circular root movements often produce development sections of continuous flow. They almost invite labeling as "expanded retransitions." While this is doubtless an exaggeration, there is nevertheless a marked contrast between their smooth continuity and the dramatic events of his expositions and recapitulations. In contrast, Haydn's developments not only show more organic construction, but their sudden pauses, stable tonal plateaus, and occasional false recapitulations all combine to create greater sectionalization. The more decisive harmonic articulation at their openings (see Chapter Three) creates an immediate formal delineation which throws them into sharper relief than Mozart's developments. Hence Haydn's developments are autonomous structures – independent formal entities with their own dramatic life – to a greater degree than Mozart's. And it is this greater formal autonomy that becomes the point of departure for a great classicist of the next generation, who, of course, grants to the development even greater significance: Ludwig van Beethoven.

Chapter Five

Recapitulation Procedures

"The classical style is a style of reinterpretation," asserts Charles Rosen. "One of its glories is its ability to give an entirely new significance to a phrase by placing it in another context."[56] If Rosen is right, then surely one of the most fruitful areas of Haydn-Mozart comparison lies in their recapitulation procedures. Far from being a static restatement of the exposition (with the simple insertion of the necessary "adjustment" to insure a tonic ending), a recapitulation is inextricably bound up with the concept of reinterpretation. Old material is often reworked, assuming new meaning through placement in different contexts.

There is of course a framework underlying the procedure, mirroring that of the exposition. Opening material in the tonic is followed by the transition, which is now altered either to remain in the tonic, or to circle back to it. What follows the adjustment (that is, the initial point of alteration) is material from the exposition's secondary and closing areas (reappearing either in full or in part), originally heard in the dominant, but now brought home to the tonic. Yet this leaves open a number of dimensions where Haydn and Mozart make quite different choices.

The most sweeping of these choices result from a stylistic practice generally avoided by Mozart but favored by Haydn: the monothematic principle. In the expositions of fully half of his movements under consideration, Haydn, upon arriving at the secondary key area, simply restates the familiar opening melody, or presents material derived from it. (Mozart adopts this practice in only one fifth of his movements.) Within the exposition itself this presents no problem, since the basic interest of sonata style lies not in its thematic contrast, but in its

56   *The Classical Style*, p. 78.

tonal opposition. But in the recapitulation, where there is of course no such opposition, the problem is obvious – redundancy, or even sheer tautology. Hence a major change must be made. And as one would expect, Haydn has several solutions.[57]

Haydn's Symphony No. 98 displays the most obvious solution: simple omission. The exposition opens with:

Haydn: Symphony No. 98, first movement

The transition duly follows:

---

[57]   For the discussion of these as seen in Haydn's later symphonies, I am indebted to Eugene K. Wolf's study, "The Recapitulations in Haydn's London Symphonies," *The Musical Quarterly*, vol. 52, no. 1, January, 1966, pp. 71-89.

Since the secondary area material is based on the opening, Haydn simply leaves it out in the recapitulation.

Yet there remains a section of closing material from the exposition, originally sounded in the dominant, which must now be brought home to the tonic. Hence an adjustment in the music is necessary. This adjustment is crucial – it marks the turning point in the large-scale conflict between tonic and dominant. The adjustment commences at bar 229:

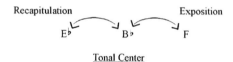

Tonal Center

The adjustment includes three critical events, each of which plays an important role in the tonal drama. First is the use of the subdominant. Appearing at measure 230 (and strengthened by the tonicizing progression which starts a bar earlier), the subdominant emphasis readjusts the listener's larger harmonic perspective. Just as the exposition had featured a move from tonic to dominant, so now the tonic is approached from its underside, or sub-dominant. This harmonic event thereby creates a Classical symmetry, as tonal equilibrium is now restored. The second event is found at measures 232-33: a progression from the dominant of the dominant to the dominant. Again, this parallels an event from the exposition. The original transition to the dominant usually "overshoots," so to speak, to the dominant of the dominant of the dominant, often appearing as a brief passing chord in first inversion.[58] Hence, the re-establishment of the tonic here a fifth lower necessitates a corresponding extension to the dominant of the dominant, once again resulting in an overall tonal balance. The third event is the conspicuous pedal point on the dominant, starting at bar 233. Its resolution at measure 238

_____

58   Technically, the transition of this movement uses the leading tone of the dominant of the dominant, which functions in the same way.

208

effectively clinches the outcome of the tonic-vs.-dominant drama.

These three events – the appearance of the subdominant, the dominant-of-the-dominant-to-dominant progression, and the dominant pedal point and tonic resolution – are what give an "adjustment" passage its characteristic sound. In Haydn's music the most conspicuous of the three is the last. For example, in the Piano Trio H. XV, No. 16, the pedal point (bar 147) is sustained for five full measures. And in the String Quartet Op. 50, No. 2, the pedal point (bar 213) is preceded by a passage (indicated by the arrow) which sounds remarkably like a development section:

Haydn: String Quartet, Op. 50, No. 2, first movement

Contrapuntal entries, thematic inversion (starting at bar 203), and dense chromaticism all duly appear. Hence the pedal point suggests the conclusion of a retransition.

In the "Military" Symphony, Haydn again solves the problem of redundancy by omitting the secondary area material. But here his choice has more drastic consequences. Just 16 bars into the recapitulation, he cuts to the closing material. At this point, a simple restatement of this material would have resulted in a disproportionately short recapitulation. Instead, Haydn interrupts the proceedings with a jarring harmonic surprise:

Haydn: Symphony No. 100 ("Military"), first movement

At first this sounds like a coda. But eventually the remaining closing material returns:

The "coda" was really a deflection, a huge insertion intruding into the closing material. Haydn uses it not only to expand the dimensions of the recapitulation, but also to create and then resolve a last surge of harmonic tension, dramatizing the final affirmation of the tonic.[59]

---

[59] In the last movement, the final resolution is dramatized in an entirely different way. As the adjustment passage draws to a close, Haydn heralds the final victory of the tonic by bringing home the secondary material with a glorious fanfare of clashing cymbals, ringing triangle and resounding bass drum (bar 265). Aside from the exhilaration created by this magnificent stroke, the passage shows Haydn, through sheer inventiveness, employing a concept that was to come to full fruition over a century later: the use of timbre to articulate major structural points – something quite familiar to us from Debussy and Webern!

One hardly needs an intimate familiarity with Mozart to sense that such procedures are alien to his style. As is well known, Mozart's recapitulations mirror his expositions far more closely than do Haydn's. His changes are mostly decorative. An example from the "Linz" Symphony will serve as an effective reminder:

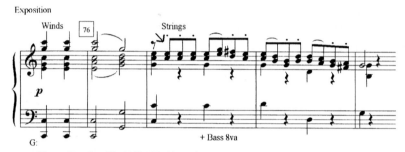

Mozart: Symphony No. 36, K. 425 ("Linz"), first movement

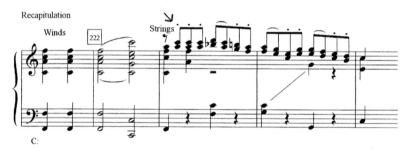

Other than this ornamental change, the recapitulation proceeds almost note for note as did the exposition.

Almost, but not quite. Mozart adds a short coda. More important, he makes the requisite harmonic adjustment in a very different way from Haydn. The original transition, in the exposition, begins:

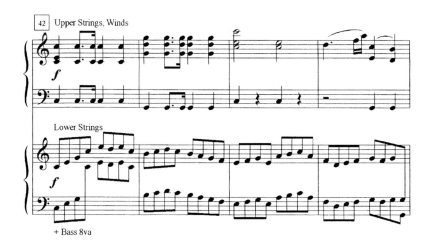

It then duly leads into the dominant. But in the recapitulation Mozart anchors the music to the tonic by stressing *his* favorite adjustment device – the subdominant:

Here the subdominant weight is effected by the tonicization and sheer repetition of the chord.

In the finale of the "Jupiter" Symphony, Mozart creates a subdominant emphasis through critical placement. The famous adjustment passage involves a chain of chromatic harmonies which sounds far-flung even to the post-Tristan harmonic sensibilities of a modern audience. To the work's first listeners, the effect must have been like entering a tonal labyrinth:

Mozart: Symphony No. 41, K. 551 ("Jupiter"), fourth movement

216

Hence the triumphant emergence of the subdominant (bars 253-54) would have sounded even more momentous at the time than it does to us today – it would have served to bring listeners back into the familiar harmonic world of the 18th century.

Illuminating in a very different way is the "Dissonant" Quartet. Here, the adjustment passage is only four bars long and includes no subdominant reference. But, as if in compensation, the subdominant harmony permeates the rest of the movement. The opening of the exposition includes a subdominant reference,

Mozart: String Quartet, K. 465 ("Dissonant"), first movement

which is further stressed at the recapitulation, where it is tonicized:

The secondary area material was originally:

218

But now it is altered to produce a subdominant emphasis:

And in the coda Mozart stresses the subdominant by tonicizing it repeatedly:

By effectively throwing harmonic weight onto the flat side of the tonic, he secures the final tonal outcome to the home key.

Obviously, Mozart had a unique capacity to create dramatic resolution through harmonic means. How does Haydn resolve his dramatic tensions as his movements approach their close? The answer is not far to seek. His String Quartet Op. 76, No. 1, has a delightful tune in its closing area. It is cited by Charles Rosen as an example of Haydn's use of the popular style, with its air of unbuttoned relaxation and its predictable, good-natured joviality:

Haydn: String Quartet, Op. 76, No. 1, first movement

Rosen points out that such tunes, insofar as they anchor the music firmly in place, function as cadential forces, to round off and to articulate the form.[60] So it comes as no surprise that when this "cadence" returns to conclude the recapitulation, it is expanded to create a greater sense of finality:

60   *The Classical Style*, p. 335.

Of course Haydn's decision to expand the form does not exclude the harmonic factor from the picture. Because of the momentary intrusion of chromaticism (bar 204) the final affirmation of the tonic sounds more deeply satisfying.

In his String Quartet Op. 54, No. 2, Haydn's expansion coincides with his adjustment passage. In the exposition, the primary key area was the scene of a jarring deflection – an unexpected and prolonged harmonic turn – as the flatted submediant intruded into the rightful sphere of the tonic:

Exposition

Haydn: String Quartet, Op. 54, No. 2, first movement

When the intrusion recurs in the recapitulation, it is expanded by a dozen bars. As in the String Quartet Op. 50, No. 2 (see pp. 209-10), the modulating sequences and concluding pedal point make the passage sound like a development section:

Recapitulation

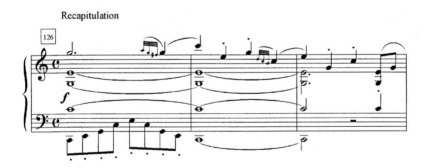

IV₆♯/IV

Expansion to underscore tonic stability

IV   VII₆   IV₆♯   II⁷

poco cresc.

piu cresc.

228

Coming after this dramatic tension and tonal instability, the peaceful tonic resolution at bar 163 is doubly effective.

More ingenious is Haydn's procedure in the String Quartet Op. 64, No. 2, a minor-mode piece. In the exposition, a deflection occurs in the customary position between the secondary and closing material. As usual, this surrounding material is in the relative major. The sudden shift to minor creates a moment of high drama:

Haydn: String Quartet, Op. 64, No. 2, first movement

In the recapitulation, Haydn faces two problems. Since the surrounding material is now already in a minor key (the tonic), how will he preserve the dramatic impact of the passage without the modal shift? Second, how will he resolve the extreme chromaticism of measures 28-30 so as to provide stability as the movement approaches its close? Haydn's solution is twofold. First, he inserts a large chunk of material into the secondary area (at bar 92), material which concludes with repeated dominant-tonic progressions anchoring the tonality firmly to the tonic. He then abridges the deflection itself (bar 98). In doing so, he combines its Neapolitan with its sequential rising melodic leaps. The combined length of the enlarged secondary area and the altered deflection totals twice that of the corresponding passage in the exposition. The formal expansion is immediately recognizable as a salient feature of Haydn's style:

How does Mozart deal with such deflections when they recur in recapitulations? In most cases, his penchant for formal symmetry prevails, resulting in a simple literal repetition. But in a few instances, a very different factor is operating.

One of Mozart's most powerful deflections is found in the "Jupiter" Symphony. The dramatic pause, the sudden tutti on the minor subdominant, and

231

the shifts between major and minor create great expressive force:

Mozart: Symphony No. 41, K. 551 ("Jupiter"), first movement

When the deflection returns in the recapitulation it is even more powerful. Again, it starts on the minor subdominant. But now, Mozart enlarges the deflection to include an additional harmonic stroke, as he proceeds farther down the flat side of the tonic to the Neapolitan:

Mozart is effectively recalling a point of harmonic tension (the minor subdominant) then moving out beyond it and bringing it home to the tonic. A visual analogy might be throwing a lasso, which requires overshooting the mark in order to bring the targeted object in. The same stroke reappears in the finale. Here, occurring within a whirlwind profusion of events in allegro molto cut time, it is less conspicuous. Yet again there is a turn to the minor subdominant in the exposition:

233

+ Bass 8va

Mozart: Symphony No. 41, K. 551 ("Jupiter"), fourth movement

iv₆

And again, in the recapitulation, there is a further move down to the Neapolitan (bar 328), here in striking 6/4 position:

Mozart is challenging the stability of the tonic by pushing the deflection out beyond its original tonal frontiers. Hence the final resolution to C major sounds more triumphant.

The most conspicuous instance of Mozart's re-working of a deflection to effect larger harmonic resolution occurs in the finale of the "Dissonant" Quartet. The closing area incorporates a sudden turn to the flatted submediant:

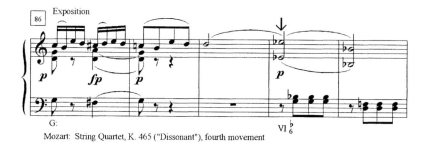

Mozart: String Quartet, K. 465 ("Dissonant"), fourth movement

When this passage returns in the recapitulation, the turn itself is diverted, again, down the flat side of the harmonic ladder to the Neapolitan (bar 308). And it stays there at some length (through bar 318). The sense of formal freedom and harmonic adventure anticipates Schubert:

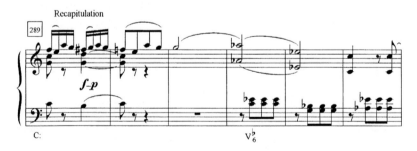

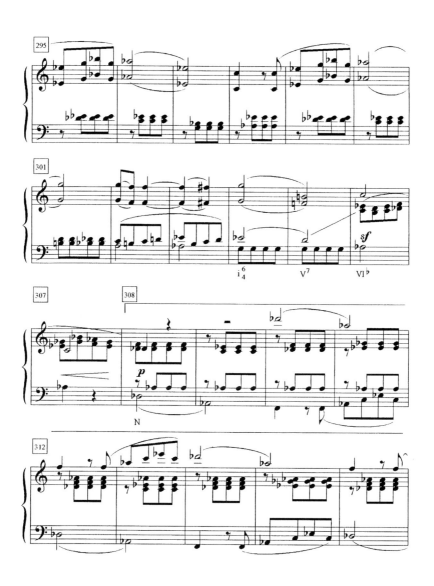

In all three of these instances, the powerful effect of Mozart's re-worked deflections results from their occurrence within larger contexts of formal symmetry. It is just because Mozart's recapitulations closely mirror his expositions that any deviations from the pattern carry greater weight.

One might ask if Haydn, in the 174 of his movements under consideration here, never alters his deflections to stress harmonic resolution rather than create formal expansion. An apparent instance occurs in his String Quartet Op. 54, No. 3. As in Mozart's "Dissonant" Quartet, the flatted submediant intrudes into the closing area. The intrusion is brief:

Haydn: String Quartet, Op. 54, No. 3, first movement

240

But in the recapitulation the deflection is indeed re-written to include a critical Neapolitan (at bar 168):

Yet there are crucial differences which set Haydn's practice apart from Mozart's. Between the flatted submediant (bar 153) and the Neapolitan (bar 168), Haydn inserts nine bars of dominant harmony (starting at 157) and a tonic resolution (at 166). And unlike Mozart, who maintains a continuous eighth-note pulse, Haydn introduces a violin solo which seems to bring the music to a halt (at 164). Hence, while Mozart's alteration preserves the deflection as a continuous passage fitting smoothly into the larger structure, Haydn's intervening tonic and his changes of sonority and rhythm imply a lesser regard for larger tonal resolution. Rather, his concern is to write a harmonic progression that sounds boldly conclusive at a local level.[61]

---

[61] In the interest of completeness, there is one case where Haydn rewrites a deflection to help resolve the larger harmonic tension. In his Symphony No. 98, the closing material includes a turn to the subtonic, or flatted leading tone; when the passage recurs in the recapitulation, Haydn further extends it to the flatted mediant – one step further down the flat side of the tonal ladder.

Mozart's sensitivity to larger tonal relationships results in a master stroke of harmonic reinterpretation, again in the "Jupiter" Symphony. In the exposition, the transition is the scene of a tremendous struggle between the two polar forces of tonic and dominant. The turning point occurs at bars 48-49:

Mozart: Symphony No. 41, K. 551 ("Jupiter"), first movement

Here the dominant is established as the new key. But in the recapitulation Mozart readjusts the transition, starting at its very beginning. Shifting to the minor, he then stresses the flat or subdominant side of the tonic:

Hence when the same struggle subsequently recurs, it appears in a different light, i.e., it is reinterpreted. Since Mozart has thrown harmonic weight onto the other side of C major, the tonic now enters the conflict at a distinct advantage, and emerges victorious. The adjustment at bar 235 (compare with 47-49) does not alter the tonal outcome so much as confirm what is already implicit in the music – the final triumph of the tonic:

Mozart's intuitive awareness of the effects of chromaticism, and of the infinite shades of emotion created by even the smallest alterations, gives his harmonic language an operatic subtlety and richness. His expressiveness often becomes especially intense as a movement draws to its close. For example, at the recapitulation of the "Haffner" Symphony Mozart shifts the closing phrase to the minor mode, creating a fleeting poignancy (compare bars 88-92 with the concluding bars 194-98). But it is the "Prague" Symphony which reveals his operatic genius at its peak. The exposition opens with:

Mozart: Symphony No. 38, K. 504 ("Prague"), first movement

The secondary area melody contains a poignant major-minor shift (see discussion of modal mixture, pp. 64-66). At the start of the recapitulation, a chromatic alteration in the accompaniment (foreshadowed earlier in the exposition's secondary area) subtly heightens the listener's awareness of unfolding drama:

248

This is only a hint of things to come. As the music approaches its close, Mozart takes a familiar motif from the exposition:

and reharmonizes it. The bittersweet chromaticism suggests an underlying pathos:

The momentum sweeps the listener along to the close, and to Mozart's crowning stroke. The closing material of the exposition already sounds powerfully affecting:

But now Mozart alters it to include a descending chromatic line (bar 286) – a small detail, but so intensely expressive as to suggest the descent of an operatic curtain on all of the preceding high drama of the movement:

250

Here Mozart is the master of the stage – the composer of *The Marriage of Figaro* (written in the same year, and in the same key) – recreating the dramatic world of opera through purely instrumental means. As always, he does so with great economy of procedure; since the changes are strictly local, the formal balance and outward serenity of the music remain unshaken.

Haydn, while lacking Mozart's extraordinary harmonic sensitivity, has his own method of indicating an approaching conclusion, one that is perhaps better suited to his more workmanlike approach: synthesis of elements. Though not a frequent occurrence, the device nevertheless reflects an essential facet of Haydn the ingenious craftsman. For example, in the last movement of his String Quartet Op. 64, No. 1, when the secondary area material returns in the recapitulation it is combined with the primary area material (starting at bar 98, last beat). His Op. 77, No. 1, concludes with a coda which combines elements of the primary and secondary areas (starting at bar 168, the tune from the opening is subjected to a descending sequence that recalls the secondary material at bar 28). More conspicuous is his procedure in the slow movement of the Symphony No. 98. The opening melody contains three rhythmic motifs – an initial half-note and quarter-note figure, a dotted-eighth and 32nd-note figure, and concluding 16th-note triplets:

Haydn: Symphony No. 98, second movement

In the coda all three motifs recur almost simultaneously, the opening figure and the triplets in combination at bar 72, and the dotted-eighth figure in stretto at bar 76:

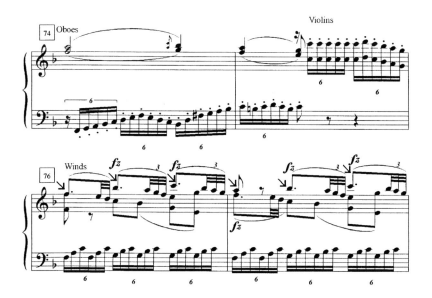

But Haydn's most arresting synthesis is found in the coda of his "Oxford" Symphony, a prime example of what Charles Rosen calls the high level of surface drama found in his music.[62] The exposition opens with a theme which contains two salient figures: a four-note rhythmic motif, and a concluding upward skip:

+ Bass 8va

Haydn: Symphony No. 92 ("Oxford"), first movement

As the movement approaches its close, Haydn combines the two figures as he leaps into a remote key – and launches a coda of overwhelming power:

---

62   *The Classical Style*, p. 185.

Even when his method is less overt, Haydn's concluding strokes are bolder than Mozart's, as if to compensate for the greater expressive richness of his younger contemporary. The recapitulation of the "Surprise" Symphony begins with the return of the opening melody supported by simple counterpoint (bar 153):

Haydn: Symphony No. 94 ("Surprise"), first movement

After the adjustment and the tonic return of the secondary area material, Haydn writes a lengthy insertion whose dominant pedal point and final cadential progression create a tremendous expansion:

255

256

At this point Haydn brings back the opening melody (bar 218). But now, an added bass line makes its tension-resolution patterns more explicit. Heard in the context of Haydn's simpler and more straightforward emotional world, the stroke is doubly effective:

Indeed, the remaining secondary and closing material which follow seem almost an afterthought.

The same device yields more dramatic results in the Symphony No. 95. Here Haydn rivals Mozart in expressive richness, if not emotional subtlety. At the very opening, a fragmentary motif is heard in stark octaves:

Haydn: Symphony No. 95, first movement

Near the end, however, Haydn not only shifts from minor to major, but fills in the octaves with full, expressive harmonies over a powerful tonic pedal point, creating an effect of apotheosis:

Haydn's penchant for such culminating effects reaches its climax in the "Drumroll" Symphony. The work opens with a mysterious-sounding introduction:

258

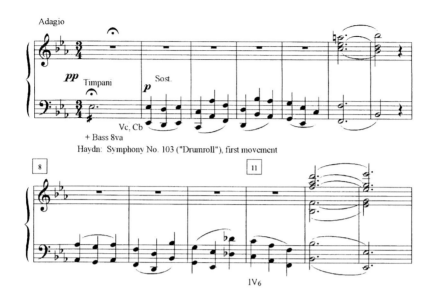

Haydn: Symphony No. 103 ("Drumroll"), first movement

Its reference to the subdominant in bar 11 foreshadows the same reference in the primary area material[63]:

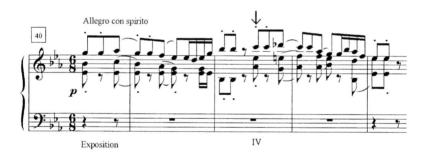

Later, its melody appears transposed as part of the transition:

[63]   Steven Haas, "Coexistent Compositional Practices in the First Movement of Gustav Mahler's Tenth Symphony" (M. A. Thesis, University of California, Los Angeles, 1977, p. 56). Haas compares the "thematic interconnections" in the Haydn movement with those in the finale of Mahler's Sixth Symphony, where such interconnections are more complex, and where "the ambiguous nature of the thematic recurrence" makes formal classification difficult.

+ Bass 8va

The recapitulation proceeds in a unusually predictable fashion (for Haydn!). An adjustment passage of only three bars results in unusual stability at this ordinarily eventful juncture:

A listener familiar with Haydn's style might well suspect that the composer is keeping in store a crucial dramatic stroke. And sure enough, a sudden shift to minor proclaims an approaching event of great importance:

The event is of course the return of the slow introduction. Not only does it provide formal unity, but it lends the music an appropriate weight as the conclusion approaches. And it represents a summit of the Classical art of reinterpretation. "[D]uring its first statement, the introduction is a kind of inchoate source for future material; when it returns it is a summary – a condensed recapitulation – of events that have already occurred."[64]

---

[64]   Op. cit., p. 57.

Haydn and Mozart approach the minor mode from different perspectives. In Mozart's minor-mode pieces, which account for eight out of his 89 movements, the recapitulations invariably remain in minor throughout. Haydn's practice is more variable. In half of his 25 minor-mode movements, he follows Mozart's procedure, altering his secondary material in the recapitulation.[65] In the remaining cases, however, Haydn shifts to the parallel major in the recapitulation, preserving his secondary area material intact. Wilhelm Fischer (in his classic 1915 study, "Zur Entwicklungsgeschichte des Wiener klassischen Stils"[66]) notes that these shifts occur in movements where Haydn's secondary material has pronounced melodic interest. Haydn presumably shifts to major, then, in order to accommodate the melody. At the same time, Haydn may have been more concerned than Mozart about the relative instability of the minor mode, and hence, in these instances, chose not to conclude with it.

Finally, as Rosen points out, Mozart's tremendous achievements in the genre of the piano concerto result from a gift which Haydn lacked: a keen instinct for the control of long-range tonal relations.[67] In his concerto recapitulations this instinct is immediately challenged by a formal problem – the handling of the "double exposition." A complete literal repetition would be out of the question: it would conflict with the dynamic nature of the Classical style. Mozart occasionally solves the problem by commencing the recapitulation with the first solo entrance (particularly in slow movements). More often, he combines the ritornello with the solo entrance material either literally, or varied (as in K. 488, starting at bar 198).

The supreme example of Mozart's large-scale harmonic control in his piano concerti is the great C-Minor Concerto, K. 491. The solo exposition alone encompasses 182 bars, and is as harmonically far-ranging as it is formally massive. The piano entrance,

---

[65]   String Quartets Op. 33, No. 1 (first and last movements), Nos. 5 and 6 (second movements), Op. 42 (first and last movements), Op. 64, No. 2, Op. 76, No. 2, Piano Trios H. XV, Nos. 12 and 26, and No. 16 (second movement), and his Piano Sonata, H. XVI, No. 34.

[66]   *Studien zur Musikwissenschaft*, II (1915), pp. 24-84.

[67]   *The Classical Style*, p. 185-86.

Mozart: Piano Concerto No. 24, K. 491, first movement

leads to primary area material that is unusually chromatic:

The customary transition leads to the secondary area:

Now Mozart launches a masterful deception. What follows sounds very much like closing figurations,

leading to the expected cadential trill and ritornello:

The ritornello's lyrical melody is then taken up by the piano in an apparent dovetailing into the development (a common enough concerto procedure). A shift

265

to the minor creates the usual instability here, paving the way for further chromatic meanderings:

Oddly enough, these meanderings soon lead back to E-flat major, and to passagework which sounds increasingly cadential:

Only at this point does the listener realize the deception: this is still the exposition, and bars 220-40 were a huge deflection. The closing material leads to a final cadential trill – and a concluding ritornello marks the genuine end of the exposition.

An exposition of such harmonic instability and chromatic tension presents a major obstacle to a final tonal resolution. Mozart of course is fully equal to the task. Rather than following the adjustment passage with material from the beginning of the secondary key area, he presents a melody that was originally heard 50 bars further along – after E-flat had been firmly established – but is now brought home to the tonic (compare the following with bars 201-4, above):

The melody's reappearance – now in the home key – settles the tonal outcome beyond any doubt. He then sounds the melody in the subdominant, then resolves it through the dominant back to the tonic, creating a large-scale cadential progression. Only then does he present the material from the beginning of the secondary area. Its built-in tonicizing progressions now serve to clinch the tonic outcome:

Finally, he simply omits the lengthy deflection, replacing it with material from the orchestral introduction.

The ways in which Haydn and Mozart recapitulate and resolve the tensions of sonata style reveal a great deal about their concepts of the style as a whole. Haydn, ever the ingenious craftsman, is a master at manipulation of form. His frequent monothematic structures run the risk of redundancy in recapitulations; his solutions to the problem involve him in sweeping changes totally unlike Mozart's more symmetrical formal conceptions. For Haydn, dramatic resolution means expansion of structure: expansion which may occur in adjustment passages, tonal deflections, or actual thematic material. And his keener sense of surface drama results in bolder strokes at his conclusions, such as combining melodic elements, or harmonizing bare melodic lines to emphasize their tension-resolution patterns.

Mozart's greater thematic variety enables him to largely sidestep the problem of monothematic recapitulations. Hence he often assigns his changes a more ornamental role. At the same time, the greater formal symmetry of his recapitulations sets the stage for his operatic feats of long-range harmonic resolution. His masterful use of the subdominant at adjustment passages provides a gentle reassurance that all issues will be resolved, that his dramatic plot will culminate in a richly satisfying dénouement. On a few occasions he creates this feeling by altering a deflection: extending the passage further down the flat side of tonal structure, he then returns home to the tonic, making it clear that all tonal

270

tensions have been resolved. In contrast to Haydn's carefully worked-out methods of creating finality at his conclusions, Mozart simply follows his harmonic instinct, creating intensely moving effects through more subtle means, such as a descending chromatic line.

The key to Haydn's concept of sonata recapitulation, then, is form. Large-scale structural changes and formal expansions are central to his procedure. With Mozart, the critical weight lies on harmony. All tensions must ultimately be stabilized, and long-range tonal balance restored, before the movement may finally come to a close.

Chapter Six

Conclusions

The distinct individual styles achieved by Haydn and Mozart while employing the identical musical grammar remain one of the great miracles of Western music. The harmonic backdrop of their styles, tonic-dominant polarity, is more vivid in Haydn. His powerful modulations (with their insistent tonicizing reiterations), and the dramatic arrivals at his secondary harmonic areas contrast sharply with Mozart. Mozart's frequent allusions back to the tonic in the dominant area (heard here as the subdominant) create a different tonal world – a world whose twin harmonic poles are closer together and where the high dramatic tension, which Haydn achieves through their elemental opposition, is diminished. In its place stands greater overall melodic contrast, a natural consequence of Mozart's more relaxed secondary material. The greater melodic expressiveness of Mozart in general is further enhanced by his frequent modal shifts, whose major-minor mixtures create the subtle poignancy found in much of his later music. The higher level of Haydn's surface drama also appears at his structural junctures. Mozart is careful to supply a harmonic pivot (whether a single chord or a progression) at the beginnings of his developments, but Haydn's modulations are frequently more abrupt. In a few striking examples, he dispenses with connective material altogether, replacing it with a stark juxtaposition of unrelated keys. Thus, he makes greater use of dramatic surprise to articulate the larger structure.

A segment of the structure which Haydn often articulates in this way – the development – is thus provided with a strong formal identity from its very outset. And the procedures that follow, unlike the continuous sequences of Mozart's developments, confirm this strong identity. Haydn's developments are distinct, sectionalized structures: sections of modulating sequences are separated by stable harmonic plateaus. While Mozart's developments reveal a heavier reliance on conventional material, Haydn's show thoroughly organic construction, often involving ingenious alterations of the thematic material. Sometimes their dramatic importance is further heightened by the Haydnesque stamp of a false recapitulation. This opens up new possibilities of formal play: at one extreme Haydn may hint at the "falseness" of the false return by making significant alterations in harmony or orchestration, while at the other he may exploit the deceptive element fully, preceding the false return with a "retransition" centered on the dominant (of the false key!).

Haydn's fondness for formal play continues throughout the recapitulation. In the exposition, his greater tonic-dominant polarity helped create dramatic tension and interest (even within a structure that was often monothematic). But now that this tonal tension has been resolved, he must make structural changes to maintain dramatic interest, or – if the piece is monothematic – simply to avoid tautology. Such changes include omission of material, reharmonization, alteration of deflections to strengthen cadential functions, and syntheses of earlier melodic and rhythmic elements. And a sense of proportion informs his adjustment passages, as they often assume the role of short developments.

Mozart remains more sensitive to long-range tonal relationships. His move to the dominant in the exposition creates a large-scale tension that remains in effect through his developments, in part because they are shorter and less eventful than Haydn's. Such tensions are worked out without Haydn's sudden key juxtapositions or false recapitulations: Mozart prefers to let the instability accumulate right up to the retransition, where a well-grounded dominant pedal point leads to a decisive tonic return. The operatic flavor of these resolutions is unmistakable.

This long-range harmonic sensitivity is even more striking in Mozart's recapitulations, perhaps because his changes, being fewer in number than Haydn's, seem to carry more weight. The prevalence of the subdominant in adjustment passages attests to a thoroughgoing concern for tonal balance and symmetry at the highest level. Finally, in several instances Mozart's practice of transforming the literal repetition of a deflection into a further digression down the flat side of tonal structure demonstrates the lengths to which he will go to make certain that *all* tensions have been resolved, just as they would be in a large-scale drama.

When these differences are placed side by side, the reasons for the identification of each composer with his most characteristic genre become clear. It is only natural that Haydn's more "intellectual" style, with its continuous formal play and thematic manipulation, should find its most perfect expression in the string quartet. It is equally inevitable that Mozart's intuitive grasp of harmony and his extraordinary sensitivity to any unresolved tonal tensions – however remote in time – should find their fulfillment in the operatic masterpieces which are among the crowning glories of the Classic period.

Note

The following bibliography is largely drawn from the entries "Joseph Haydn" and "Wolfgang Amadeus Mozart" in *The New Grove Dictionary of Music and Musicians*, Second Edition, edited by Stanley Sadie (Executive Editor, John Tyrell), London: Macmillan, 2001. The compiler of the Haydn bibliography is James Webster; the authors of the Mozart entry are Cliff Eisen and Stanley Sadie. All of the entries dealing with works covered in this book have been included.

Bibliography

Abert, H.: "Joseph Haydns Klavierwerke," *Zeitschrift für Musikwissenschaft,* ii (1919-20)

Adler, G.: "Haydn and the Viennese Classical School," *The Musical Quarterly,* xviii (1932), 191-207

Autexier, P.A.: *Les oeuvres témoins de Mozart* (Paris, 1982)

Badura-Skoda, E.: "The Influence of the Viennese Popular Comedy on Haydn and Mozart," *Proceedings of the Royal Musical Association,* c (1973-4), 185-99

Ballstaedt, A.: "'Humor' und 'Witz' in Joseph Haydns Musik," *Archiv für Musikwissenschaft,* lv (1998), 195-219

Bandur, M.: *Form und Gehalt in den Streichquartetten Joseph Haydns: Studien zur Theorie der Sonatenform* (Pfaffenweiler, 1988)

Bard, R.: "'Tendenzen' zur zyklischen Gestaltung in Haydns Londoner Sinfonien," *Gesellschaft für Musikforschung Kongressbericht* [1950-]: *Bayreuth 1981,* 379-83

Bard, R.: *Untersuchungen zur motivischen Arbeit in Haydns sinfonischem Spätwerk* (Kassel, 1982)

Bartha, D.: "Mozart et le folklore musical de l'Europe centrale," *Les influences étrangères dans l'oeuvre de W. A. Mozart: Paris 1956,* 157-81

Bartha, D.: "Thematic Profile and Character in the Quartet Finales of Joseph Haydn (a Contribution to the Micro-Analysis of Thematic Structure)," *Studia Musicologica Academiae Scientiarum hungaricae,* xi (1969), 35-62

Bartha, D.: "Volkstanz-Stilisierung in Joseph Haydns Finale-Themen," *Festschrift für Walter Wiora,* ed. L. Pinscher and C.-H. Mahling (Kassel, 1967), 375-84

Beck, H.: "Harmonisch-melodische Modelle bei Mozart," *Mozart-Jahrbuch des Zentralinstituts für Mozartforschung* [1950-] *1967,* 90-99

Benary, P.: "Die langsamen Einleitungen in Joseph Haydns Londoner Sinfonien," *Studien zur Instrumentalmusik: Lothar Hoffmann-Erbrecht zum 60. Geburtstag,* ed. A. Bingmann and others (Tutzing, 1988), 239-51

Benary, P.: "Metrum bei Mozart: zur metrischen Analyse seiner letzten drei Sinfonien," *Studien zur Musikzeitung/Revue musicale suisse,* cxiv (1974), 201-5

Blume, F.: "Joseph Haydns künstlerische Persönlichkeit in seinen Streichquartetten," *Jahrbuch der Musikbibliothek Peters 1931*, 24-48; repr. in idem: *Syntagma musicologicum: gesammelte Reden und Schriften* (Kassel, 1963), 526-51

Bonds, M.E.: "The Sincerest Form of Flattery? Mozart's 'Haydn' Quartets and the Question of Influence," *Studi musicali*, xxii (1993), 365-409

Bonds, M.E.: "The Symphony as Pindaric Ode," *Haydn and his World*, ed. E. Sisman (Princeton, NJ, 1997), 131-53

Bonds, M.E.: *Haydn's False Recapitulations and the Perception of Sonata Form in the Eighteenth Century* (diss., Harvard U., 1988)

Brauner, J.: *Studien zu den Klaviertrios von Joseph Haydn* (Tutzing, 1995)

Broder, N.: "Mozart and the 'Clavier,' " *The Musical Quarterly*, xxvii (1941), 422-32; repr. in P.H. Lang, ed.: *The Creative World of Mozart* (New York, 1963/R), 76-85

Broder, N.: "The Wind-Instruments in Mozart's Symphonies," *The Musical Quarterly*, xix (1933), 238-59

Brown, A.P.: "Critical Years for Haydn's Instrumental Music: 1787-90," *The Musical Quarterly*, lxii (1976), 374-94

Brown, A.P.: "The Structure of the Exposition in Haydn's Keyboard Sonatas," *The Music Review*, xxxvi (1975), 102-29

Brown, A.P.: "The Sublime, the Beautiful and the Ornamental: English Aesthetic Currents and Haydn's London Symphonies," *Studies in Music History Presented to H. C. Robbins Landon*, ed. O. Biba and D. W. Jones (London, 1996), 44-71

Brown, A.P.: *Joseph Haydn's Keyboard Music: Sources and Style* (Bloomington, IN, 1986)

Bruce, I.M.: "A Note on Mozart's Bar-Rhythms," *The Music Review*, xvii (1956), 35-47

Brück, M.: *Die langsamen Sätze in Mozarts Klavierkonzerten: Untersuchungen zur Form und zum musikalischen Satz* (Munich, 1994)

Bushler, D.: "Harmonic Structure in Mozart's Sonata-Form Developments," *Mozart-Jahrbuch des Zentralinstituts für Mozartforschung* [1950-] *1984-85*, 15-24

Caplin, W.E.: *Classical Form: A Theory of Formal Functions for the Instrumental Music of Haydn, Mozart, and Beethoven* (New York, 1998)

Caplin, W.E.: "The 'Expanded Cadential Progression': A Category for the Analysis of Classical Form," *Journal of Musicological Research*, vii (1987), 215-57

Cherbuliez, A.-E.: "Bemerkungen zu den 'Haydn' Streichquartetten Mozarts und Haydns 'Russischen' Streichquartetten," *Mozart-Jahrbuch des Zentralinstituts für Mozartforschung* [1950-] *1959*, 28-45

Chua, D.: "Haydn as Romantic: a Chemical Experiment with Instrumental Music," *Haydn Studies,* ed. W. D. Sutcliffe (Cambridge, 1998), 120-51

Cobin, M.W.: "Aspects of Stylistic Evolution in Two Mozart Concertos: K. 271 and K. 482," *The Music Review,* xxxi (1970), 1-20

Cole, M.S.: "Haydn's Symphonic Rondo Finales: their Structural and Stylistic Evolution," *Haydn Yearbook 1982,* 113-42

Cole, M.S.: "The Rondo Finale: Evidence for the Mozart-Haydn Exchange?" *Mozart-Jahrbuch des Zentralinstituts für Mozartforschung* [1950-] *1968-70,* 242-56

Cushman, D.S.: *Joseph Haydn's Melodic Materials: an Exploratory Introduction to the Primary and Secondary Sources together with an Analytical Catalogue and Tables of Proposed Melodic Correspondence and/or Variance* (diss., Boston U., 1972)

Danckwardt, M.: *Die langsame Einleitung: ihre Herkunft und ihr Bau bei Haydn und Mozart* (Tutzing, 1977)

Danuser, H.: "Das Ende als Anfang: Ausblick von einer Schlussfigur bei Joseph Haydn," *Studien zur Musikgeschichte: eine Festschrift für Ludwig Finscher,* ed. A. Laubenthal and K. Kusan-Windweh (Kassel, 1995), 818-27

David, H.T.: "Mozartean Modulations," *The Musical Quarterly,* xlii (1956), 162-86; repr. in P.H. Lang, ed.: *The Creative World of Mozart* (New York, 1963/R), 76-85

David, J.N.: *Die Jupiter-Symphonie: eine Studie über die thematischmelodischen Zusammenhänge* (Göttingen, 1953, 4/1960)

Davis, S.G.: "Harmonic Rhythm in Mozart's Sonata Form," *The Music Review,* xxvii (1966), 25-43

de Saint-Foix, G.: *Les symphonies de Mozart* (Paris, 1932; Eng. trans., 1947/R)

Dearling, R.: *The Music of Wolfgang Amadeus Mozart: the Symphonies* (London and Rutherford, NJ, 1982)

Dickinson, A.E.F.: *A Study of Mozart's Last Three Symphonies* (London, 1927/R, 2/1939)

Dunhill, T.F.: *Mozart's String Quartets* (London, 1927/R)

Edwards, G.: "Papa Doc's Recap Caper: Haydn and Temporal Dyslexia," *Haydn Studies,* ed. W.D. Sutcliffe (Cambridge, 1998), 120-51

Edwards, G.: "The Nonsense of an Ending: Closure in Haydn's String Quartets," *The Musical Quarterly,* lxxv (1991), 227-54

Einstein, A.: "Mozart's Choice of Keys," *The Musical Quarterly,* xxvii (1941), 415-21

Einstein, A.: "Mozart's Ten Celebrated String Quartets," *The Music Review,* iii (1942), 159-69

Eisen, C. and Seiffert, W.-D., eds.: *Mozarts Sreichquintette: Beiträge zum musikalischen Satz, zum Gattungskontext und zu Quellenfragen* (Stuttgart, 1994)

Eisen, C.: "Another Look at the 'Corrupt Passage' in Mozart's G minor Symphony K. 550: its Sources, 'Solution' and Implications for the Composition of the Final Trilogy," *Early Music,* xxv (1997), 373-81

Eisen, C.: "New Light on Mozart's 'Linz' Symphony, K. 425," *Journal of the Royal Musical Association,* cxiii (1988), 81-96

Eisley, I.R.: "Mozart and Counterpoint: Development and Synthesis," *The Music Review,* xxiv (1963), 23-29

Engel, H.: "Haydn, Mozart und die Klassik," *Mozart-Jahrbuch des Zentralinstituts für Mozartforschung* [1950-] *1959,* 46-79; another version in *International Musicological Society Congress Report* [1930-] *VII: New York 1961,* i, 285-304

Engel, H.: "Mozarts Instrumentation," *Mozart-Jahrbuch des Zentralinstituts für Mozartforschung* [1950-] *1956,* 51-74

Engel, H.: "Nochmals: thematische Satzverbindungen und Mozart," *Mozart-Jahrbuch des Zentralinstituts für Mozartforschung* [1950-] *1962-3,* 14-23

Feder, G.: "Bemerkungen über die Ausbildung der klassischen Tonsprache in der Instrumentalmusik Haydns," *International Musicological Society Congress Report* [1930-] *VIII: New York 1961,* i, 305-13

Feder, G.: "Eine Methode der Stiluntersuchung, demonstriert an Haydns Werken," *Gesellschaft für Musikforschung Kongressbericht* [1950-]: *Leipzig 1966,* 275-85

Feder, G.: "Similarities in the Works of Haydn," *Studies in Eighteenth-Century Music: a Tribute to Karl Geiringer,* ed. H.C.R. Landon and R.E. Chapman (New York and London, 1970), 186-97

Federhofer, H. and others: "Tonartenplan und Motivstruktur (Leitmotivtechnik?) in Mozarts Musik," *Idomeneo Conference: Salzburg 1973* (*Mozart-Jahrbuch des Zentralinstituts für Mozartforschung* [1950-] *1973-4*), 82-144 [discussions]

Feldman, M.: "Staging the Virtuoso: Ritornello Procedure in Mozart, from Aria to Concerto," in N. Zaslaw, ed.: *Mozart's Piano Concertos: Text, Context, Interpretation* (Ann Arbor, 1996)

Finscher, L.: "Joseph Haydn und das italienische Streichquartett," *Analecta musicologica* (some vols. in series *Studien zur italienisch-deutschen Musikgeschichte*), Veröffentlichungen der Musikabteilung des Deutschen historischen Instituts in Rom (Cologne, 1963-), no. 4 (1967), 13-37

Finscher, L.: *Joseph Haydn und seine Zeit* (Laaber, 2000)

Fischer, W.: "Zur Entwicklungsgeschichte des Wiener klassischen Stils," *Studien zur Musikwissenschaft,* iii (1915), 24-84

Fisher, S.C.: "Further Thoughts on Haydn's Symphonic Rondo Finales," *Haydn Yearbook 1992,* 85-107

Fisher, S.C.: *Haydn's Overtures and their Adaptations as Concert Orchestral Works* (diss., U. of Pennsylvania, 1985)

Forman, D.: *Mozart's Concerto Form: the First Movements of the Piano Concertos* (London, 1971/R)

Garland, J.: "Form, Genre, and Style in the Eighteenth Century Rondo," *Music Theory Spectrum*, xvii (1995), 27-52

Georgiades, T.: "Zur Musiksprache der Wiener Klassiker," *Mozart-Jahrbuch des Zentralinstituts für Mozartforschung* [1950-] *1951*, 50-60

Gerlach, S.: "Haydns Orchesterpartituren: Fragen der Realisierung des Texts," *Haydn-Studien*, v/3 (1984), 169-83

Girdlestone, C.M.: *Mozart et ses concertos pour piano* (Paris, 1939; Eng. trans., 1948, 3/1978)

Grave, F.K.: " 'Rhythmic Harmony' in Mozart," *The Music Review*, xli (1980), 87-102

Gwilt, R.: "Sonata-Allegro Revisited," *In Theory Only*, vii/5-6 (1984), 3-33

Haimo, E.: "Haydn's Altered Reprise," *Journal of Music Theory*, xxxii (1988), 335-51

Haimo, E.: *Haydn's Symphonic Forms: Essays in Compositional Logic* (Oxford, 1995)

Harrison, B.: *Haydn: the 'Paris' Symphonies* (Cambridge, 1998)

Harutunian, J.: "Haydn and Mozart: Tonic-Dominant Polarity in Mature Sonata-Style Works," *The Journal of Musicological Research*, ix/4 (1990), 273-98

Hepokoski, J.: "Beyond the Sonata Principle," *Journal of the American Musicological Society*, LV/1 (2002), 91-154

Hess, E.: "Die 'Varianten' im Finale des Streichquintettes KV. 593," *Mozart-Jahrbuch des Zentralinstituts für Mozartforschung* [1950-] *1960-61*, 68-77

Heuss, A.: "Das dämonische Element in Mozarts Werken," *Zeitschrift der Internationalen Musik-Gesellschaft*, vii (1905-6), 175-86

Hodgson, A.: *The Music of Joseph Haydn: the Symphonies* (London, 1976)

Hoyt, P.A.: "Haydn's 'False Recapitulations,' Late-Eighteenth-Century Theory, and Modern Paradigms of Sonata Form." Unpublished paper presented to the Department of Music, Yale University, 30 March 2001

Hümmeke, W.: *Versuch einer strukturwissenschaftlichen Darstellung der ersten und vierten Sätze der zehn letzten Streichquartette von W.A. Mozart* (Münster, 1970)

Hunter, M.: "Haydn's London Piano Trios and his Salomon String Quartets: Private vs. Public?" *Haydn and his World*, ed. E. Sisman (Princeton, NJ, 1997), 103-30

Hutchings, A.: *A Companion to Mozart's Piano Concertos* (London, 1948, 2/1950/R)

Irving, J.: *Mozart's Piano Sonatas: Contexts, Sources, Styles* (Cambridge, 1997)

Irving, J.: *Mozart: the 'Haydn' Quartets* (Cambridge, 1998)

Jan, S.B.: *Aspects of Mozart's Music in G minor: toward the Identification of Common Structural and Compositional Characteristics* (New York, 1995)

Josephson, N.S.: "Modulatory Patterns in Haydn's Late Development Sections," *Haydn Yearbook 1992*, 181-91

Kamien, R. and Wagner, N.: "Bridge Themes within a Chromaticized Voice Exchange in Mozart Expositions," *Music Theory Spectrum*, xix (1997), 1-12

Kecskeméti, I.: "Opernelemente in den Klavierkonzerten Mozarts," *Mozart-Jahrbuch des Zentralinstituts für Mozartforschung* [1950-] *1968-70*, 111-18

Keefe, S.: "Koch's Commentary on the Late Eighteenth-Century Concerto: Dialogue, Drama and Solo/Orchestral Relations," *Music and Letters*, lxxix (1998), 368-85

Keefe, S.: "The Stylistic Significance of the First Movement of Mozart's Piano Concerto No. 24 in C minor, K. 491: a Dialogic Apotheosis," *The Music Review*, xviii (1999), 1-37

Keller, H.: "KV. 503: the Unity of Contrasting Themes and Movements," *The Music Review*, xvii (1956), 48-58, 120-29

Keller, H.: "The Chamber Music" in *The Mozart Companion*, ed. H.C.R. Landon and D. Mitchell (London and New York, 1956/R), 90-137

Keller, H.: *The Great Haydn Quartets: their Interpretation* (London, 1986)

Kerman, J., ed.: *W.A. Mozart: Piano Concerto in C Major, K. 503* (New York, 1970) [score and essays]

Kerman, J.: "Mozart's Piano Concertos and their Audience," *On Mozart: Washington DC 1991*, 151-68

King, A.H.: "Mozart's Counterpoint: its Growth and Significance," *Music and Letters*, xxvi (1945), 12-20

King, A.H.: *Mozart Chamber Music* (London, 1968)

Komlós, K.: "Haydn's Keyboard Trios Hob. XV: 5-17: Interaction between Texture and Form," *Studia Musicologica Academiae Scientiarum hungaricae*, xxviii (1986), 351-400

Konold, W.: "Normerfüllung und Normverweigerung beim späten Haydn am Beispiel des Streichquartetts op. 76, nr. 6," *Joseph Haydn: Cologne 1982*, 54-73

Krones, H.: " 'Meine Sprache versteht man durch die ganze Welt': das 'redende Prinzip' in Joseph Haydns Instrumentalmusik," *Wort und Ton im europäischen Raum: Gedenkschrift für Robert Schollum*, ed. H. Krones (Vienna, 1989), 79-108

Krones, H.: "Das 'hohe Komische' bei Joseph Haydn," *Österreichische Musikzeitschrift*, xxxviii (1983), 2-8

Krummacher, F.: "Klaviertrio und sinfonischer Satz: zum Adagio aus Haydns Sinfonie Nr. 102," *Quaestiones in musica: Festschrift für Franz Krautwurst*, ed. F. Brusniak and H. Leuchtmann (Tutzing, 1989), 325-35

Landon, H.C.R.: "The Concertos, II: their Musical Origin and Development," *The Mozart Companion,* ed. H.C.R. Landon and D. Mitchell (London and New York, 1956/R), 234-82

Landon, H.C.R.: *The Symphonies of Joseph Haydn* (London, 1955) [incl. thematic catalogues of authentic, spurious and doubtful syms., pp. 605-823]; suppl. (London, 1961)

Larsen, J.P.: "The Symphonies," *The Mozart Companion,* ed. H.C.R. Landon and D. Mitchell (London and New York, 1956/R), 156-99

Larsen, J.P.: "Zu Haydns künstlerischer Entwicklung," *Festschrift Wilhelm Fischer,* ed. H. von Zingerle (Innsbruck, 1956), 123-29; Eng. trans. in Larsen (C1988)

Leisinger, U.: *Joseph Haydn und die Entwicklung des klassischen Klavierstils bis ca. 1785* (Laaber, 1994)

Lorenz, F.: *W.A. Mozart als Clavier-Componist* (Breslau, 1866)

Lowinsky, E.E.: "On Mozart's Rhythm," *The Musical Quarterly,* xlii (1956), 162-86; repr. in Lang, B1963, 31-55

Lüthy, W.: *Mozart und die Tonartencharakteristik* (Strasbourg, 1931/R)

Martinez-Göllner, M.L.: "Joseph Haydn: Symphonie Nr. 94," *Meisterwerke der Musik,* xvi (Munich, 1979)

Marx, K.: "Über thematische Beziehungen in Haydns Londoner Symphonien," *Haydn-Studien,* iv/1 (1976), 1-19

Marx, K.J.: *Zur Einheit der zyklischen Form bei Mozart* (Stuttgart, 1971)

Massenkeil, G.: *Untersuchungen zum Problem der Symmetrie in der Instrumentalmusik W.A. Mozarts* (Wiesbaden, 1962)

McClary, S.: "A Musical Dialect from the Enlightenment: Mozart's Piano Concerto in G major, K. 453, Movement 2," *Cultural Critique,* iv (1986), 129-69

Mercado, M.R.: *The Evolution of Mozart's Pianistic Style* (Carbondale, IL, 1992)

Meyer, L.: "Grammatical Simplicity and Relational Richness: the Trio of Mozart's G minor Symphony," *Critical Inquiry,* ii (1975-6), 693-761

Mitchell, W.J.: "Giuseppe Sarti and Mozart's Quartet K. 421," *Current Musicology,* no. 9 (1969), 147-53

Neubacher, J.: "'Idee' und 'Ausführung': zum Kompositionsprozess bei Joseph Haydn," *Archiv für Musikwissenschaft,* xli (1984), 187-207

Neubacher, J.: *Finis coronat opus: Untersuchungen zur Technik der Schlussgestaltung in der Instrumentalmusik Joseph Haydns, dargestellt am Beispiel der Streichquartette* (Tutzing, 1986)

Newman, S.T.M.: "Mozart's G minor Quintet (KV. 516) and its Relationship to the G minor Symphony (KV. 550)," *The Music Review,* xvii (1956), 287-303

Newman, W.S.: "Haydn as Ingenious Exploiter of the Keyboard," *Joseph Haydn: Vienna 1982,* 43-53

Noske, F.: "Le principe structural génétique dans l'oeuvre instrumental de Joseph Haydn," *Revue belge de musicologie,* xii (1958), 35-39

Nowak, L.: "Die Skizzen zum Finale der Es-dur-Symphonie GA 99 von Joseph Haydn," *Haydn-Studien,* ii/3 (1970), 137-66

Palm, A.: "Mozarts Streichquartett d-moll, KV 421, in der Interpretation Momignys," *Mozart-Jahrbuch des Zentralinstituts für Mozartforschung* [1950-] *1962-3,* 256-79

Paul, S.E.: *Wit, Comedy and Humour in the Instrumental Music of Franz Joseph Haydn* (diss., U. of Cambridge, 1981)

Pfann, W.: " 'Einbescheidener Platz in der Sonatenform...': zur formalen Gestaltung des Menuetts in den Haydn-Quartetten Mozarts," *Archiv für Musikwissenschaft,* lii (1995), 316-36

Plath, W. and others: "Typus und Modell in Mozarts Kompositionsweise," *Idomeneo Conference: Salzburg 1973* (*Mozart-Jahrbuch des Zentralinstituts für Mozartforschung* [1950-] *1973-4*), 145-78 [discussions]

Powers, H.S.: "Reading Mozart's Music: Text and Topic, Sense and Syntax," *Current Musicology,* no. 57 (1995), 5-44

Raab, A.: *Funktionen des Unisono, dargestellt an den Streichquartetten und Messen von Joseph Haydn* (Frankfurt, 1990)

Ratner, L.: *Classic Music: Expression, Form, and Style* (New York, 1980)

Ratner, L.: "Harmonic Aspects of Classic Form," *Journal of the American Musicological Society* (1949), 159-68

Rosen, C.: *Sonata Forms* (New York, 1980, 2/1988)

Rosen, C.: *The Classical Style: Haydn, Mozart, Beethoven* (London and New York, 1971, enlarged 3/1997 with sound disc)

Rosenberg, R.: *Die Klaviersonaten Mozarts: Gestalt und Stilanalyse* (Hofheim, 1972)

Salzer, F.: "Haydn's Fantasia from the String Quartet, Opus 76, No. 6," *Music Forum,* iv (1976), 161-94

Sandberger: "Zur Geschichte des Haydn'schen Streichquartetts," *Altbayerische Monatsschrift,* ii (1900), 41-64; rev. in *Ausgewählte Aufsätze zur Musikgeschichte,* i (Munich, 1921/R), 224-65

Saslav, I.: *Tempos in the String Quartets of Joseph Haydn* (diss., Indiana U., 1969)

Schenker, H.: "Haydn: Sonate C Dur" [H XVI: 50], *Der Tonwille,* ii (1923), 15-18

Schenker, H.: "Haydn: Sonate Es Dur" [H XVI: 52], *Der Tonwille,* i (1922), 3-21

Schenker, H.: "Mozart: Sinfonie g-moll," *Das Meisterwerk in der Musik,* ii (Munich, 1926/R), 105-57; Eng. trans. (Cambridge, 1996), 59-96

Schenker, H.: "Vom Organischen der Sonatenform," *Das Meisterwerk in der Musik,* ii (Munich, 1926/R), 43-54; Eng. trans., *Journal of Music Theory* xii (1968) [H. XVI: 44, first movement]

Schlager, J.H.: *Joseph Haydn: Sinfonie Nr. 104 D-dur,* Meisterwerke der Musik, xxxvii (Munich, 1983)

Schmalzriedt, S.: "Charakter und Drama: Zur historischen Analyse von Haydnschen und Beethovenschen Sonatensätzen," *Archiv für Musikwissenschaft,* xlii (1985), 37-66

Schmid, E.F.: "Mozart and Haydn," *The Musical Quarterly,* xlii (1956), 145-61

Schrade, L.: "Joseph Haydn als Schöpfer der klassischen Musik," *De scientia musicae studia atque orationes,* ed. E. Lichtenhahn (Berne, 1967), 506-18

Schröder, G.: "Über das 'klassische Orchester' und Haydns späte symphonische Instrumentation," *Musik-Konzepte,* no. 41 (1985), 79-97

Schroeder, D.P.: *Haydn and the Enlightenment: the Late Symphonies and their Audience* (Oxford, 1990)

Schwarting, H.: "Ungewöhnliche Repriseneintritte in Haydns späterer Instrumentalmusik," *Archiv für Musikwissenschaft,* xvii (1960), 168-82

Schwindt-Gross, N.: *Drama und Diskurs: zur Beziehung zwischen Satztechnik motivischem Prozess am Beispiel der durchbrochenen Arbeit in den Streichquartetten Haydns und Mozarts* (Laaber, 1989)

Sechter, S.: "Analysis of the Finale of Mozart's Symphony no. 41 in C (K. 551, 'Jupiter') (1843)," *Music Analysis in the Nineteenth Century, i: Fugue, form and style,* ed. I. Bent (Cambridge, 1993), 79-96

Sechter, S.: *Das Finale der Jupiter-Symphonie (C dur) von W.A. Mozart,* ed. F. Eckstein (Vienna, 1923)

Seiffert, W.D.: "Mozart's 'Haydn' Quartetts: an Evaluation of the Autographs and First Edition, with Particular Attention to mm. 125-42 of the Finale of K. 387," in C. Eisen, ed.: *Mozart Studies 2* (Oxford, 1997), 175-200

Shanmgar, B.: "Rhythmic Interplay in the Retransitions of Haydn's Piano Sonatas," *Journal of Musicology,* iii (1984), 55-68

Siegmund-Schultze, W.: *Mozarts Melodik und Stil* (Leipzig, 1957)

Sisman, E.: "Genre, Gesture, and Meaning in Mozart's 'Prague' Symphony," in C. Eisen, ed.: *Mozart Studies 2* (Oxford, 1997), 27-84

Sisman, E.: *Haydn and the Classical Variation* (Cambridge, MA, 1993)

Sisman, E.: *Mozart: The 'Jupiter' Symphony* (Cambridge, MA, 1993)

Somfai, L.: " 'Ich war nie ein Geschwindschreiber...': Joseph Haydns Skizzen zum langsamen Satz des Streichquartetts Hoboken III: 33," *Festskrift Jens Peter Larsen,* ed. N. Schiørring, H. Glahn and C.E. Hatting (Copenhagen, 1972), 275-84

Somfai, L.: " 'Learned Style' in Two Late String Quartet Movements of Haydn," *Studia musicologica Academiae scientiarum hungaricae,* xxviii (1986), 325-49

Somfai, L.: "The London Revision of Haydn's Instrumental Style," *Proceedings of the Royal Musical Association,* c, (1973-4), 159-74

Somfai, L.: "Vom Barock zur Klassik: Umgestaltung der Proportionen und des Gleichgewichts in zyklischen Werken Joseph Haydns," *Jahrbuch für österreichische Kulturgeschichte,* ii: *Joseph Haydn und seine Zeit* (1972), 64-72

Somfai, L.: *Joseph Haydn zongoraszonátái: hangszerválasztás és eloadói gyakorlat, mufaji tipológia és stílselemzés* (Budapest, 1979; Eng. trans., with C. Greenspan, 1995, as *The Keyboard Sonatas of Joseph Haydn: Instruments and Performance Practice, Genres and Styles)*

Sondheimer, R.: *Haydn: a Historical and Psychological Study based on his Quartets* (London 1951)

Spitzer, M.: "Haydn's Reversals: Style Change, Gesture and the Implication-Realization Model," *Haydn Studies,* ed. W.D. Sutcliffe (Cambridge, 1998) 177-217

Spitzer, M.: "The Retransition as Sign: Listener-Oriented Approaches to Tonal Closure in Haydn's Sonata Form Movements," *Journal of the Royal Musical Association,* cxxi (1996), 11-45

Sponheuer, B.: "Haydns Arbeit am Finalproblem," *Archiv für Musikwissenschaft,* xxxiv (1977), 199-224

Steinbeck, W.: "Mozart's 'Scherzi': zur Beziehung zwischen Haydns Streichquartetten op. 33 und Mozarts Haydn-Quartetten," *Archiv für Musikwissenschaft,* xli (1984), 208-31

Steinberg, L.: *Sonata Form in the Keyboard Trios of Joseph Haydn* (diss., New York U., 1976)

Strohm, R.: "Merkmale italienischer Versvertonung in Mozarts Klavierkonzerten," *Mozart und Italien: Rom 1974, [Analecta musicologica* (some vols. in series *Studien zur italienisch-deutschen Musikgeschichte),* Veröffentlichungen der Musikabteilung des Deutschen historischen Instituts in Rom (Cologne, 1963-), no.18 (1978)], 219-36

Subotnik, R.R.: "Evidence of a Critical World View in Mozart's Last Three Symphonies," *Music and Civilisation: Essays in Honor of Paul Henry Lang,* ed. E. Strainchamps, M.R. Maniates and C. Hatch (New York, 1984), 29-43

Sutcliffe, W.D.: *Haydn: String Quartets, op. 50* (Cambridge, 1992)

Sutcliffe, W.D.: *The Piano Trios of Haydn* (diss., U. of Cambridge, 1989)

Szabolcsi, B.: "Die 'Exotismen' Mozarts," *Leben und Werk W.A. Mozarts: Prague, 1956,* 181-88; Eng. trans., *Music and Letters,* xxxvii (1956), 323-32

Tepping, S.E.: *Fugue Process and Tonal Structure in the String Quartets of Haydn, Mozart, and Beethoven* (diss., Indiana U., 1987)

Therstappen, H.J.: *Joseph Haydn sinfonisches Vermächtnis* (Wolfenbüttel, 1941)

Tischler, H.: *A Structural Analysis of Mozart's Piano Concertos* (Brooklyn, NY, 1966)

Toeplitz, J.: *Die Holzbläser in der Musik Mozarts und ihr Verhältnis zur Tonartwahl* (Baden-Baden, 1978)

Tovey, D.F.: "Franz Joseph Haydn," *Cobbett's Cyclopedic Survey of Chamber Music*, i (London, 1929-30, 2/1963/R), 514-48; repr. as "Haydn's Chamber Music," *Essays and Lectures on Music* (London, 1943), 1-64

Tovey, D.F.: "Haydn: Pianoforte Sonata in E flat, No.1," [H XVI: 52] *Essays in Musical Analysis: Chamber Music* (London, 1944/R), 93-105

Tovey, D.F.: *Essays in Musical Analysis* (London, 1935-44/R)

Tovey, D.F.: *Essays in Musical Analysis* (London, 1935-9), i, iii, vi [incl. Essays on orchestral works]

Tovey, D.F.: *Essays in Musical Analysis: Chamber Music,* ed. H.J. Foss (London, 1944/R)

Treitler, L.: "Mozart and the Idea of Absolute Magic," *Das musikalische Kunstwerk: Festschrift Carl Dahlhaus,* ed. H. Danuser and others (Laaber, 1988), 413-40; repr. in *Music and the Historical Imagination* (Cambridge, MA, 1989), 176-214

van der Meer, J.H.: "Die Verwendung der Blasinstrumente im Orchester bei Haydn und seinen Zeitgenossen," *Der junge Haydn: Graz 1970*, 202-20

Vertrees, J.A.: "Mozart's String Quartet K. 465: the History of a Controversy," *Current Musicology,* no.17 (1974), 96-114

Walter, H.: "Zum Wiener Streichquartett der Jahre 1780 bis 1800," *Haydn-Studien,* vii/3-4 (1998), 289-314

Weber-Bockholdt, P.: "Joseph Haydns Sinfonien mit langsamen ersten Sätzen," *Die Musikforschung,* xlv (1992), 152-61

Webster, J.: "Are Mozart's Concertos 'Dramatic'? Concerto Ritornellos versus Aria Introductions in the 1780s," in N. Zaslaw, ed.: *Mozart's Piano Concertos: Text, Context, Interpretation* (Ann Arbor, 1996)

Webster, J.: "On the Absence of Keyboard Continuo in Haydn's Symphonies," *Early Music,* xviii (1990), 599-608

Wheelock, G.A.: *Haydn's Ingenious Jesting with Art: Contexts of Musical Wit and Humor* (New York, 1992)

Willner, C.: "Chromaticism and the Mediant in Four Late Haydn Works," *Theory and Practice,* xiii (1988), 79-114

Winkler, G.J.: "Opus 33/2: zur Anatomie eines Schlusseffekts," *Haydn-Studien,* vi/4 (1994), 288-97

Wolf, E.K.: "The Recapitulations in Haydn's London Symphonies," *The Musical Quarterly,* lii (1966), 71-89

Wolf, E.K.: "The Rediscovered Autograph of Mozart's Fantasy and Sonata in C minor, K. 475/457," *Journal of Musicology,* x (1992), 3-47

Wollenberg: "The Jupiter Theme: New Light on its Creation," *The Musical Times,* cxvi (1975), 781-83

Zaslaw, N., ed.: *Mozart's Piano Concertos: Text, Context, Interpretation* (Ann Arbor, 1996)

Zaslaw, N.: "Mozart, Haydn and the *sinfonia da chiesa*," *Journal of Musicology*, i (1982), 95-124

Zaslaw, N.: *Mozart's Symphonies: Context, Performance Practice, Reception* (Oxford, 1989)

Index

adjustment passages
  attributes 2, 208-9
  in Haydn 185, 192, 206-10, 225, 260, 270, 274
  in Mozart 212-23, 247, 270, 274
  and sonata style 24
  and tonic-dominant conflict 206, 208-9
  and tonic return 2, 24, 201, 209
altered (re-worked) deflection. *See under* tonal deflections
altered transition. *See* adjustment
Anderson, Emily 150n
Bach, Johann Sebastian 21
Baroque era, music of 5, 21, 50
  and sonata style 8
Baroque ritornello principle 50
Beethoven, Ludwig van 10
  Fifth Symphony 141, 163n
  Ninth Symphony 183
  "Eroica" Symphony *177-78*
  "Pastoral" Symphony 46
  developments, autonomy of 176-79, 199
  tonic-dominant polarity in 24, 141
Bernstein, Lawrence 34n
bifocal close
  attributes 34
  in Haydn 35, 38
  in Mozart 32-35, 38, 73
  and polarity, effect on 38
  and sonata style 73
Blume, Friedrich
  on Mozart and Haydn 3-4, 5n
Brahms, Johannes 183
Bruckner, Anton 183
breaks, sectional. *See* structural junctures
chromaticism
  in Haydn 25, 29, 100, 182, 210, 225, 230
  and modulation 89, 100, 106
  in Mozart 7, 57, 127, 130, 215, 248-50, 263, 266, 268, 271
circle of fifths 153, 175
circular root movement 41n, 150, 153, 199

Classic harmonic progression 41
Classic Music: Expression, Form and Style.
  See Ratner
Classical style
  and dissonance, structural 24, 141
  dramatic character of 9, 21, 24, 55, 141, 262
  formal divisions in 105
  harmony and form in 5, 6, 105
  operatic character of 24, 55, 183
  and reinterpretation 7, 201, 261
  scholarly accounts of 3-10
  symmetry in 208
  tonal deflection in 55
  see also sonata style
Classical Style, The. See Rosen
closing area material
  and elision 121, 124
  and organic developments, in Haydn 167, 173, 179
  in sonata-style movements 1, 2, 201
  and tonic return 2
  See also exposition
coda, in sonata style movements 2, 125n
compositional priorities, at structural junctures 106-10
  See also structural junctures
Cone, Edward T. 6n
continuity, at structural junctures. *See* tonal continuity
Debussy, Claude 211n
deflections. *See* tonal deflections
development procedures 11, 135-99
  false recapitulation 182-83
  in Haydn 4-5, 134, 160, 163, 179, 199, 273-74
  and monothematicism 4
  in Mozart 4-5, 8, 116, 135, 141, 154, 160, 199, 273-74
  organic developments, in Beethoven 176-79

294

296

297

false. *See* false recapitulation
  in Haydn 5, 7, 125n, 183, 201-2, 206,
    254, 262, 270-71, 274
  in minor-mode movements 262
  and monothematicism 201-2, 270, 274
  in Mozart 5, 7, 9, 125n, 201, 212, 240,
    262, 270-71, 274
  procedures 11, 201-71
  and reinterpretation 201
  in sonata-style movements 1, 2, 8, 24,
    105, 110, 201
  and tonic return 2, 9, 24, 105, 183, 201
repertoire, list of 13-20
resolution, of tension. *See* tension and
  resolution
retransitions
  dominant 130, 132, 133
  expanded, in Mozart 9, 199
  false. *See under* false recapitulation
  in Haydn 124, 125, 130n, 132-34
  in Mozart 127, 130, 133-34, 274
  non-dominant 124, 130-34
  and pedal point 125, 127
  and recapitulations 2, 10-11, 125
  and resolution, of tension 124, 130n, 133-
    34
  and sequence, descending 125
  and tonic return 2
  See also development-recapitulation
    break; non-dominant retransitions;
    tonic return
retransposition passage. *See* adjustment
  passages
re-worked (altered) deflection. *See under* tonal
  deflections
ritornello
  in Mozart 51, 53, 56, 78, 262, 265, 268
  principle, and piano concerto 50
Romantic root progression 41
Romantic style 4, 41, 131
  and false recapitulation 183
  Romantic theme transformation 38
  and sonata form 6
rondo, and Haydn 124
Rosen, Charles 51
  The Classical Style 6, 8, 9, 24n, 41n,
    179n, 224n
  Sonata Forms 8, 9
  on Classical sonata style 1, 6-8, 9, 201
  on Haydn, and surface drama 253
  on Haydn-Mozart differences 6-9, 46n,
    262
  on Mozart, and opera 6-7

on popular style, in Haydn 223

Scarlatti, Domenico, music of
  Sonata in D, L. 415 *21-23*
  as harbinger of sonata style 9, 21-24
  and tonic-dominant polarity 24
Schubert, Franz 9, 131, 238
  "Unfinished" Symphony 183
Schumann, Robert
  Op. 44 (Piano Quintet), sequences in 140-
    41
secondary key area. *See* exposition; secondary
  material
secondary material
  in Haydn 4, 5, 42, 86, 89, 91, 201, 210,
    251, 262, 273
  and minor dominant. *See* minor dominant
  and modal shifts 103
  in Mozart 4, 5, 8, 62, 75, 86, 103, 201,
    262, 273
  in recapitulation 2
  and Romantic period 183
  in sonata-style movements 1-2, 201
  and tonal deflections 55, 62, 86, 102, 229
  and tonic return 2, 201
  See also exposition
section breaks (junctures). *See* structural
  junctures
sequences
  in Beethoven 176-79
  as development procedures 1, 135
  in Haydn 95, 160-63, 173-76, 189, 273
  in Mozart 73, 125, 127, 135-60, 199, 273
  prevalence of, in 19th century 140-41
  at retransitions 125
  themes within sequential block 154-60
  and tonic-dominant polarity 141
slow movements
  developments in 182n
  in Haydn and Mozart 6, 13-20, 262
  and structural elisions 121-22
  tonic-dominant polarity in 32
sonata form 6, 8, 9
  see also sonata style
Sonata Forms. See Rosen
sonata-rondo 2n
sonata style
  and adjustment, harmonic 2, 24, 201
  attributes 1-2, 8, 9, 10-11, 24, 105, 110,
    141, 201-2
  and bifocal close 34, 73
  as continuous development 11
  development procedures 10, 11

300